Don L. Jardine, Ph.D.

♦

COMBAT MARINE at Seventeen

104 TRUE STORIES
BEFORE, DURING & AFTER WORLD WAR II

*"If every life were a book,
Dr. Jardine's life would be a library."*

CombatMarineAt17.com

Copyright © 2013 by East Bench Publishing LLC
All rights reserved.

No copyright claimed on the contemporary photographs of the war. These were photographs taken by the Marine Corps and distributed in packets to the author and other combat Marines serving in the same campaigns, when returning home after the War.

The chapter entitled "Charles 'Sparky' Schulz, creator of 'Peanuts'" is an excerpt from an article written by the author in *The Illustrator*, Summer/Fall 1985, vol. 8 no. 2, page 4, reprinted with permission from the copyright holder, Art Instruction Schools, Inc., Minneapolis, Minnesota © 1985.

Published by
East Bench Publishing
932 S 950 E
Ephraim, Utah 84627

First Edition

ISBN: 978-0-9896745-0-8
Library of Congress Control Number: 2013944608

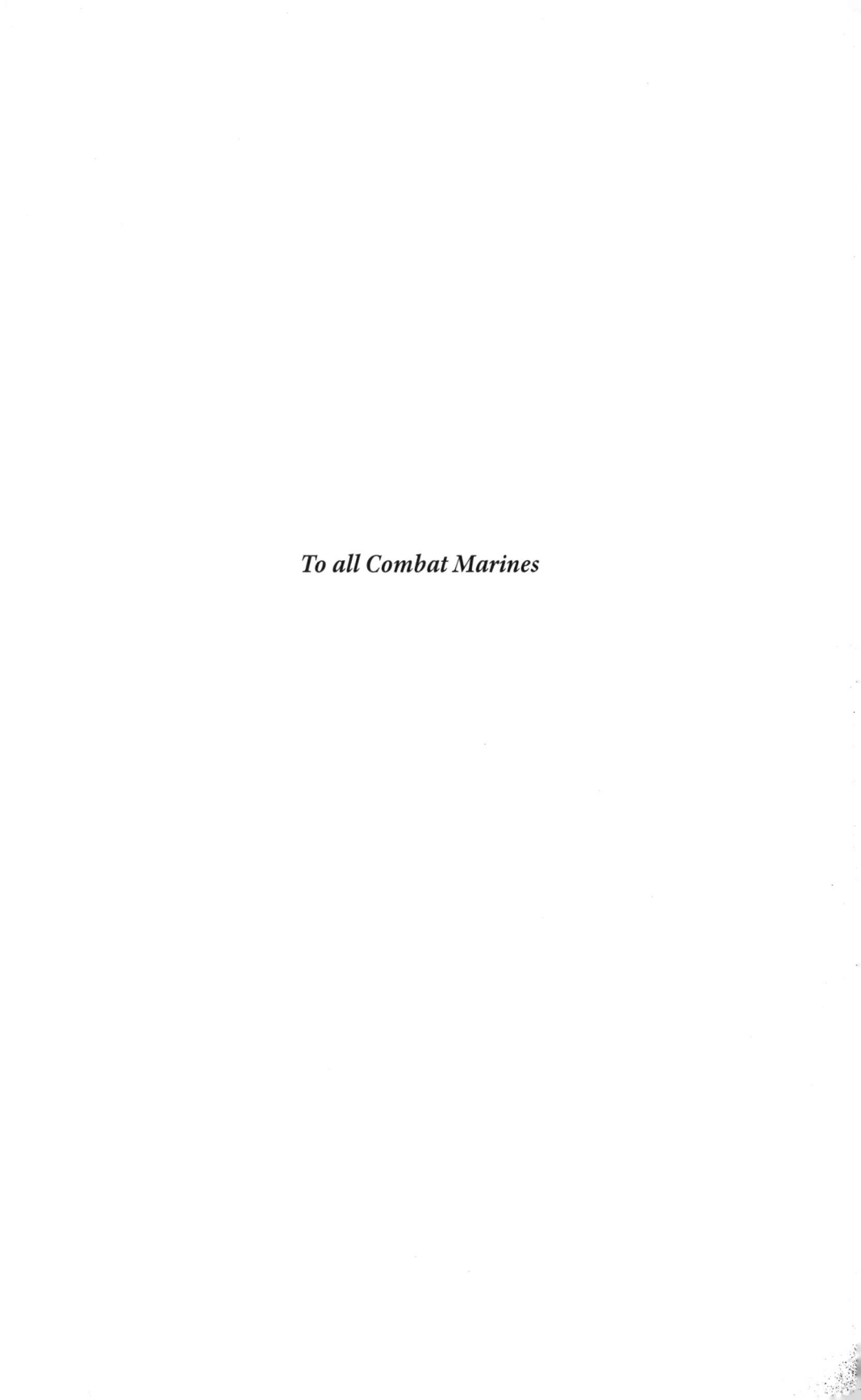

To all Combat Marines

Acknowledgments

◆

You wouldn't be reading this book if it weren't for my fine son-in-law and attorney-at-law, Ted Meikle. He typed, edited, formatted, and made corrections to the text; scanned my drawings, the original documents, and the Marine Corps photos; photographed the keepsakes; wrote the back cover text; and created the cover based on my design sketch.

Ted's wife and my wonderful daughter, Jill Meikle, and their daughters Katy and Christina assisted in several ways, including typing and proofreading. Ted and Jill's son Mark Meikle, their daughter Carol-Marie Rowley, her husband Matt Rowley, and my daughter-in-law Julie Jardine proofread the copy. Ted and Jill's children Robert Meikle and Annette Hudson added encouragement during the many years I worked on this project.

My sons Jon Tod and Kent Lee and his family encouraged me to record some wartime experiences we all hope will never again be necessary.

Brother-in-law Dr. Don C. Wood, a combat Marine in World War II wrote the flattering Foreword.

Stephen Widmer generously loaned his expensive, professional scanning equipment, letting us keep it for the better part of a year, to scan all the photographs and illustrations.

I extend apologies to any whose names are unmentioned, but thank them—and humbly dedicate this book to all Combat Marines. *Semper Fidelis.*

Table of Contents

Acknowledgments..v
Table of Contents..vi
Illustrations by the Author...xi
Photographs and Documents...xiii
FOREWORD..XVII
AUTHOR'S INTRODUCTION..XIX
    Casualties of WWII..xxvii
BEFORE WORLD WAR II..1
    I Learned to Swim..2
    Fire Ants..3
    Keyhole Snowdrift..4
    Over the Wires and through the Snow..............................5
    Airplane in Town..6
    Migrating Indians...8
    Train versus Tanker Truck..10
    Fourth of July Stampede...11
    Fishing Amid Rattlesnakes...12
    Snake Show...13
    Skiing and Arrowheads...15
    Indian Guests and Gold..16
    The Butcher Shop..18
    Idaho Potatoes 5 Cents...19
    Rigby Water Tower..20
    Schools in Rigby...21

Trapping and Hockey on the Canals............................24
Young Driver..26
Attacked by a Golden Eagle...27
Aerial Balloonist...29
Ram Attack..31
Bouncing Ball Lightning...33
Big Black Stallion..34
High School Luck..36
Shot during a Pheasant Hunt......................................39

DURING WORLD WAR II..41
December 7, 1941—Pearl Harbor Bombed................42
Move To Ogden..43
A New House at Sixteen!..46
New Job...47
Hungry for my First Flight..50
The Royal Canadian Air Force....................................52
Enlistment—U.S. Marine Corps..................................54
Boot Camp...55
Camp Pendleton...59
Hawaiian Tattoos..61
Tokyo Rose..62
Four from Rigby High School.....................................64
Eniwetok—Ships and Sharks Galore!........................66
Bombardment of Saipan..67
"And I Died for You Today, my Friend..."................68
Apprehension...70
Going Ashore—Tinian..72
Wounded—First Purple Heart....................................78
Saipan Hospital..82
To Tinian and Back..84

Amnesia—Six Lost Days..86
Saved by the Enemy...89
Souvenir Patrol...91
Ordered to Rifle Company...97
Enemy Caves...99
Wet Combat Patrol...101
Thinking of War..104
The Ninety-day Wonder...111
Forgotten Guard..114
Okinawa Invasion...117
Precious Water..119
A Saipan Patrol, and Pondering the Planes................122
Booby Trap Explosion..126
A Booby Trap Detected..128
Cold Combat Patrol..133
Barefoot Marine..135
English Speaking Japanese Prisoner............................138
"Torpedo Juice"...143
Rations and Flies..146
Timmons Revenge Patrol...148
In the Sugar Cane—The Most Dramatic
Scene of my Life...151
Enemy Encampment..157
Blinded by Enemy Hand Grenade—Second Purple
Heart..159
Jap Air Raids...164
Jo Jo and the Giant Tarantula......................................166
A Huge Bowl of Jello..168
Combat Swimming with Sharks..................................169
Same Day, Same Month, Different Year.....................177
Pinup Art...181

B-29 Bomber Missing over Japan..................................183
AFTER WORLD WAR II...187
    On a Ship to Japan...188
    In Japan: Nagasaki after the A-Bomb........................192
    Inspecting a Japanese Freighter.................................205
    A Hike through the Nagasaki Atomic Bomb Area......207
    A War Crime..210
    Coming Home..212
    Henry Patton and the Bataan Death March................216
    Thoughts on the Atomic Bombs.................................218
    Back to School...221
    Big Spence and the Wild Goose.................................225
    The Professor's Coat..230
    Mr. J. C. Penney Himself...232
    The Unforgettable Lecture...234
    Dr. Collett and the Math Teacher...............................236
    The Professor's Daughter...239
    How I Met an Angel...242
    Piloting a Stinson "Flying Station Wagon"................245
    An Unmilitary View of Saipan...................................252
    Nightmares...253
    Shots Fired...255
    Trophy Buck..258
    A Job Recommendation that Changed Everything....262
    Charles "Sparky" Schulz, creator of "Peanuts"..........266
    Judging of Art..269
    Determination! Art Competition
    for the Handicapped..271
    Who's Flying a Jet T-33? Me!....................................273
    The King's Opening Night...279

Grandpa!..282
Girl's Second-Choice Date..283
Conclusion..287

Illustrations by the Author

Airplane in town! "Once around Rigby, only $5.00."...................6

Indian woman with travois and dog...8

I didn't kill the snakes if it wasn't necessary..............................12

"After the show, you may take one snake home with you."..........13

At the butcher's..18

On the water tower in Rigby, Idaho..20

Jim Thorpe dancing at Rigby High School lyceum.....................22

Dad fishing on the Snake River..26

There was no balloon ascent that year......................................30

The stinky ram..31

The horse went under the clothesline. I didn't! The wire became the bowstring. I was the arrow..35

Cave under flat rocks..91

We set up base camp on a Saipan ridge. Looking to the north, we could see the tents of the 8th Marine regiment. I did this drawing from the west end of our camp, as a visual record censors would approve. Note the ocean in the upper right-hand corner............97

Japanese soldier...140

Japanese soldier and mate. He bowed!....................................155

Blinded by grenade..160

xi

Jo Jo eating his tarantula treat..*167*

Close encounter with the great white shark..........................*175*

Diving directly from Heaven was a U.S. Air Force P-38 twin-boomed fighter plane, its guns blazing..........................*179*

Pinup girl..*181*

Pinup girl..*182*

Pinup girl..*182*

Japanese girl, atomic bomb survivor, playing baseball with a baby on her back..*194*

I sketched this typical building while I was serving in Nagasaki after the atomic bomb..*203*

My illustrations of fraternity and sorority houses at University of Utah..*223*

"These hands don't do anything the mind doesn't tell them to do."
....*238*

Envelope to Miss Carol Wood, 1949..*243*

Envelope to Miss Carol Wood, 1950..*244*

My angel and me..*244*

Pirate and Princess..*284*

Photographs and Documents

───────── ♦ ─────────

All photographs of Saipan and Tinian campaigns and of Nagasaki atomic bomb area were taken by official U.S.M.C. photographers.

My first day of school..4
ID badge for Utah Quartermaster Supply Depot.................44
Don Jardine ID at Hill Air Force Base.....................................47
Don Jardine's dog tags...54
"And I died for you today, my friend...On an Island called Saipan..."...68
Japanese soldier's belt of a thousand stitches.......................71
Marines approach Tinian beach in Higgins landing boat..........74
"We were there. And we were Marines. This is what we trained for."...75
Tanks landing on Tinian beach..77
Certificate awarding Purple Heart for wounds received at Tinian, Marianas Islands, July 28, 1944....................................79
Going ashore at Tinian..80
Enemy casualties in burned-out sugarcane field....................80
Marines advancing in the Tinian jungle..................................81

Transporting a wounded Marine to the "hospital"....................81
Order prohibiting souvenir hunting in restricted areas of island 96
Enemy soldier in foxhole, killed by flamethrower....................100
Marine encounters Japanese family..105
Saipan's Charan Kanoa sugar factory remnants.
Note the narrow gauge train tracks...107
Disabled American tanks and enemy corpses........................108
Mail call: Infrequent, but always welcome.............................108
Flame-throwing tanks help Marines destroy enemy opposition 109
The fight moves over Jap soldiers where they fell.....................109
Marine shelter halves (small 2-man tents) and killed enemies in the aftermath of a Jap Banzai attack..110
Garapan, Saipan's capitol, destroyed by naval and aerial bombardments...110
Title page of Japanese Phrase Book issued by the USMC.........142
Blowflies and maggots infest bodies of fallen Jap soldiers........147
Sugar cane field on Saipan..152
Newspaper clipping: "Instructor on Saipan"...........................172
Swimming Instructor Certificates issued by Marine Corps and by Navy..176
Canal in Nagasaki at low tide. At night, during high tide, victims of the atomic bomb were placed in this canal, to be carried out to sea as the tide went out...190
Shrines like this remained along a walkway we followed when hiking around and through the rubble of Nagasaki................191

Rickshaws in Japan..*195*

Joseph P. Frankowski (left) and Don Jardine, in the Mariamamachi District of Nagasaki, with two young Japanese men..*196*

Japanese family business...*197*

Detail from League of Nations tapestry.....................................*198*

Metal infrastructure leans away from the atomic explosion.....*199*

Steel drapes like wet spaghetti from the bomb's intense heat....*200*

Remains of Catholic Church doorway in Nagasaki after the atomic bomb blast...*200*

Before the atomic bomb exploded, this Nagasaki canal was surrounded by large buildings...*201*

I walked the sidewalk shown on the right side of the photo many times. This was at the extreme eastern edge of Nagasaki's bomb blast area. Ahead lay a few unharmed businesses shielded from the explosion by a small hill...*202*

Japanese family moving their belongings in a handcart...........*204*

Japanese woman carrying salvaged lumber..............................*204*

Flag given to me by captain of merchant vessel after I searched his ship..*206*

At a break during our hike through the atomic bomb area, some Marines sat on heavy machinery, suffering severe radiation burns...*208*

My notes from an evening with my friend Henry Patton, Bataan Death March survivor..*217*

Marines honor their fallen...*219*

There but for the grace of God go I..220
Proud new pilot with Aeronca...222
Ready to board the Air Force T-33 trainer jet for a flight over the Great Salt Lake Desert..274
Photo I took from T-33 trainer jet of three F-101 Air Force Jets over the Great Salt Lake Desert...278

FOREWORD

By Dr. Don C. Wood, Ph.D.

Dr. Jardine, Ph.D, with meritorious military service, leads the reader through the quagmire of deadly hand-to-hand combat. His mastery of language is so creative the reader can almost smell the gun powder he describes.

He understands the personal emotion of feeling deserted by God and man. He, with countless other young Marines, finds himself wounded, in blood-soaked fox holes forged by war's destructive forces. They wonder, will help ever arrive. As fears related to loneliness creep in, a powerful motto that had been burned in his memory opens the door of hope. *Semper Fidelis. Semper Fidelis.* Always faithful. Help will come.

His personal experiences in Nagasaki, Japan, were so vivid they need no description or comment.

Dr. Jardine's direction in life is evident from the exciting stories he shares of his young years. He leaves one wondering if this part of his life was but training for all that happened later. His formal military training seemed so sketchy for one headed to battle. Certainly, the majestic mountains in his Idaho back yard provided excellent strength building opportunities. The same background developed the skills that later helped him shoot accurately at moving targets.

We are fortunate to have such a scholar as Dr. Jardine whose memory is so active and complete.

You will find it difficult to lay this book aside. You will find events of your own life buried in its pages. I urge you to read and become a "combat Marine."

Dr. Don C. Wood, Ph.D.

Upon request, my brother-in-law, Dr. Don C. Wood, wrote this foreword. Unlike myself, Dr. Wood is a humble man, never prone to recount his own experiences and achievements. Dr. Wood was also a combat Marine. He was with a reconnaissance team of Marines that went ashore by rubber raft from a submarine in the middle of a very dark night to acquire pre-invasion military information for the assault on Saipan.

During the two days and nights he and his team were on that mission, they were surrounded by enemy Japanese. They spent nights in caves and were discovered the night before re-boarding the submarine. They survived the hand-to-hand combat that followed and still met their rendezvous safely, with the vital information they were sent to obtain.

While in the Corps, Don Wood met a beautiful female Marine, Geneal Lundgren, and they married after the war.

My son Jon Tod also served in the Marines. We are a Marine Corps family.

Author's Introduction

If you enjoy true adventure short stories, I promise you will love this book.

You will read experiences I lived during World War II, and also interesting true stories from before and after the war.

- Have you ever been strafed by an enemy plane?
- Have you ever been blinded? By an enemy hand grenade?
- Have you seen, heard and smelled a human being on fire?
- Have you ever killed anyone?
- Have you ever had someone beg you to end their life?
- Have you swum with sharks? A great white shark?

- Have you walked through the site of an atomic bomb blast?
- Have you seen adults with babies and children in their arms leap to their death to avoid capture?
- Have you been aboard a ship in the middle of a deadly mine field?
- Have you witnessed an attacking kamikaze plane diving directly at you and your ship? Then lifting over your ship's deck to sink the ship beyond you?
- Have you stood guard duty, alone, for 28 hours in an isolated place surrounded by a dark jungle, strange sounds (and perhaps enemy soldiers)?
- Have you drunk from a stream, and filled your canteens, then found bleeding bodies upstream?
- Have you ever been absolutely alone many thousands of miles from home?
- Have you had gangrene from a shrapnel wound and faced amputation?
- Have you been aboard an airplane—loaded with injured Marines—that came within inches of crashing on takeoff after hitting an enemy bomb hole in the runway?
- Have you ever had a fever that robbed you of your memory, and disoriented you alone in enemy jungles for days?
- Have you cried when you saw good friends killed or badly injured?
- Have you been on a ship during a storm so severe that the captain sent out S.O.S. signals?

- Have you hidden under damp vegetation surrounded by enemies speaking in their foreign tongue?
- Have you ever been in a military field hospital "ward" (tent) on a folding cot that sank several inches into the mud, tended by an army truck driver and an army cook? For 28 days?
- Have you ever been so tired, so exhausted, you felt you had no control over yourself?
- Have you ever tried to sleep, curled around the base of a tree, when mosquitoes were sucking your blood?
- Do you know the odor of rotting human flesh? Was it nearby? Were you eating at the time? Can you still smell it?
- Have you ever watched as an enemy hand grenade flew through the air toward you? Did it explode between you and a friend, less than six feet away?
- Have you ever piloted a small airplane in a blizzard? After dark? With no radio?
- Have you ever flown into a box canyon, unable to climb over the mountain ahead, unable to land or to turn left or right? (and there is no reverse on an airplane!)
- Have you ever been attacked, repeatedly, by a huge golden eagle? (And you were 12 years old!)
- Has a wild ram ever tried to gore you with his huge curved horns?
- Have you walked on snow drifts over telephone wires?

- Have you ever, as a child, hidden behind your mother's skirts as migrating Indians, unable to speak English, begged for food?
- Have you ever held your breath under water so long you thought your lungs would burst before you could reach the surface?
- Have you ever, as a ballroom bouncer, had to fight four people at a time? Was the city mayor watching? Did he then hire you to be the city marshal?
- Has a teenage driver of a stolen car tried to run you over? Were you shooting at the car?

These stories, and other true adventures, are described in this book.

Where were you and what were you doing at age 17? and 18? and 19? Playing football, baseball, basketball? Cruising in your car? Dating? Watching television?

I was learning to use a variety of hand grenades (concussion, thermite, fragmentation); to hit distant targets with an M1 rifle, a .45 caliber pistol, a .30 caliber machine gun; how to fire a bazooka and use a flame thrower, etc. All of which would better enable me to kill people.

I have two Purple Hearts, and qualified for more. I served more than two years in the Marine Corps, was 17 years old when I first experienced combat, and was honorably discharged after the war, while still in my teens. That was not unique. Many of my fellow Marines were younger than I, but I had full confidence in their abilities to do what was necessary while we were under fire from enemy Japanese.

Yet at that same age, on leave from advanced training at Camp Pendleton and wearing my Marine uniform, I was denied admittance to a movie because it was too violent! And many years later, on a cruise ship with my wife, I saw a sign that said, "Passengers must be 21 to play Bingo!" It still bothers me to hear anyone 17 years old referred to as "a child." In combat, I soon learned that an enemy killed by a seventeen-year-old Marine is just as dead as one killed by someone older.

This is not exclusively a blood and guts book. Although it includes several of my most memorable combat experiences as a Marine during World War II, I've shared stories about a fascinating boyhood in Idaho (hunting, fishing, Indians, rattlesnakes, trapping) and stories about adventures while piloting airplanes after World War II.

Frankly, I've tried, as best I am able, to forget the sights, sounds, smells, and fears experienced in combat—ships firing big guns, airplanes (theirs and ours) dropping bombs, enemy fighter planes strafing with all their machine guns firing as we clawed into the earth beneath us, small arms and machine guns firing from concealed positions, and the screams of dying Japanese and of friends who were the unlucky ones.

As a plus, the primitive conditions under which we often lived overseas have helped me to really appreciate a clean, cold drink, a fresh water shower, a comfortable bed with clean, cool sheets, the variety of good foods available in my refrigerator, the peace and quiet of my home (without mosquitoes) etc. We have many wonderful things too often unappreciated, taken for granted without thought.

It is still a joy for me to make my own decisions, having the freedom to do what I want to do, go where I want to go when I want to, even to be what I want to be. Those things are not the military way.

To those of you who have never been in combat, I truly and sincerely wish I had the words to describe for you how fortunate you are to be able to enjoy your life without the mental baggage carried by all combat veterans. Some—more than others—still live with vivid experiences that relate closely to the imaginations of writers for television and movies. We lived it!

World War II hasn't ended. And it won't as long as a combat veteran remains among the living.

No words can let you know what it is like to await your turn to go down the side of a ship rolling in heavy seas, hanging onto a cargo net while descending as rapidly as possible to the small, heaving landing boats that will carry you onto a beach crisscrossed with fire from friendly and enemy guns, exploding mortar shells and bombs. You know that adventure and perhaps injury or even death is awaiting.

Even at my advanced age (I am completing this book at age 87) I still have nightmares that awaken me in a cold sweat. I clearly recall the terrible sounds and smells, explosions that feel like blows to the ears and the body, the whole world shaking as guns and bombs blast men and machines, smoke and cordite filling the air, burning the eyes and filling the lungs with each tortured breath.

Yes, there was excitement—but with a fear you'll never experience at any amusement park or in any movie or television show.

Mix these things with the knowledge that home is thousands of miles away, that you know only a few dozen of the thousands of young men with whom you are sharing these feelings, with the terror of projectiles whistling past you (hopefully) and exploding near you (inevitably).

Close your eyes and try to get a small taste, a visual image, of how different all of these things are compared to your life at age 17. Can you feel those bullets whistling past you? Do those huge naval guns impact your eardrums? How about the omnipresent fear of injury—or death? Can you taste it? Smell it? And is there any appreciation for the senselessness of what surrounds you? Hundreds of ships and boats carrying young men whose main purpose in life is taking the lives of other young men wearing a different uniform, speaking another language, crouching behind concealment or cover in an attempt to remain alive or uninjured, and probably just as frightened as you are. They too are far from home. They too have the same feelings and concerns.

But you don't worry about them, or even much about those around you. It's your world. Your danger. Your excitement and anticipation. Yes, anticipation. You don't know what to expect as you wade through the warm, blood-colored surf. What will be your fate? How will you perform? Which friends will you lose? What will tomorrow bring? Or—will there even be a tomorrow?

I was no hero, but I knew many who were. I am proud to have served with them. We were like brothers, and I am still saddened for the families of those who did not survive. I wish I could tell all of them so—but most have now passed on, and we're told that more than a thousand World War II veterans die in the United States *every day*. Soon, we will all be history. The fears and sacrifices of so many, in all branches of the service and all theaters of war will only be located in libraries, mostly in books that will be covered with dust because how many of our fellow Americans have any interest in history? Do they care that we fought for them as well as for ourselves?

I pray that the old axiom—history repeats itself—will not prove true regarding World War II. It hasn't yet. The Korean War and Vietnam War came closest. By far. But warfare is changing. Battlefields won't always be on the other side of the world. The loss of the Twin Towers in New York City proves that. And the horrors of war or terrorism will be experienced by countless people in the future—not all will be young men.

It is important for my readers to know one thing about the Marines in World War II. We were all under orders to refrain from keeping journals or diaries or any written records. And unlike the other branches of the military, in the Marines the possession of a camera was a general-court-martial offense. So, as you read accounts by other military personnel, full of details concerning where they were, their means of transportation, conversations, experiences, names of men with whom they served, dates, and photos they took with their own cameras, remember that they were not under the restrictions imposed upon Marines.

I have relied on my 87-year-old memory and on notes jotted down since my service, to provide that which is in this book. I trust and believe it is accurate, though frustratingly incomplete.

And, it is all true. I lived it—*and still do!*

Casualties of WWII [1]

◆

USA Military War Deaths
(to June 2013)

Afghanistan	2,229
Iraq	4,488
Korea	36,516
Vietnam	58,209
World War II	**405,399**

Percentage of People in Each Military Branch Suffering Fatalities in WWII

0.8% of the Coast Guard [2]
1.5% of the Navy[3]
2.5% of the Air Force
2.8% of the Army
3.66% of the Marine Corps

Worldwide Deaths from World War II

Total military deaths	22 to 30 million
Total civilian deaths	38 to 55 million
Total deaths	60 to 85 million

---

1 Source: Wikipedia.com "World War II casualties," and "United States military casualties of war," accessed June 24, 2013.
2 Some with Marines as Motor Macs, involved in beach landings.
3 Some with Marines as Motor Macs during landings and some attached to Marines as Corpsmen.

Before World War II

I Learned to Swim

My family was visiting our grandparents Jardine in Lewisville, Idaho one extremely hot summer day. It was suggested we all go to the nearby canal for a cool, refreshing swim.

Local aunts, uncles, and cousins were called to join us and they responded.

I was five years old and hadn't yet learned to swim, so I sat on a small bridge soaking my feet in the clear, cold rushing water. Several among the group, all of whom were good swimmers, taunted and jeered, daring me to jump in and join them. Some were near my age.

Dad stood in the center of the canal with water flowing over his shoulders (and he was six feet tall).

I had watched the frivolity for some time and envied the fun they were having, splashing and dunking each other. So, when Dad called for me to jump in, saying "I'll catch you." I did. But he didn't say *when* he would catch me.

Dad kept backing away. I learned to swim.

Years later in the South Pacific, I watched islanders toss their infants less than a year old into deep ocean waters. They swam!

I was told that babies swim intuitively. However, when they reach about two years of age most develop a fear of water, then must re-learn to swim.

Fire Ants

◆

My family was visiting our grandparents Jardine and my younger brother Max and I went tree climbing for entertainment.

We'd been climbing less that five minutes when we both began experiencing excruciating pain. We were under attack, simultaneously, by red ants! Perhaps a thousand, on cue, began biting. They had waited until we had many hundreds of them in our pant legs, then they dealt fire. Pain!

Max and I screamed in agony, and adults came running from the house. They ripped our clothes off and we jumped in the cold water of a nearby irrigation ditch. That helped, but many ants just continued to bite until we rubbed them from our tortured flesh. It was one of the most painful experiences we ever endured.

And—there is no doubt in my mind—ants communicate. In this case, maliciously!

Keyhole Snowdrift

♦

It was an especially severe winter when I was in first grade. The snow was deep and the wind nearly blew me over as my dad walked with me to the elementary school. He preceded me, trying to make a path through two feet of snow.

When we reached the school, there were only a half dozen students waiting at the front door for the principal to unlock it. He arrived when we did. Holding a big key, he unlocked the door but could hardly push it open, because the wind had blown snow through the keyhole and there was a pile of snow more than three feet high on the floor inside the door!

School wasn't held that day. The principal arranged for a bobsled, filled with clean straw, to return to their homes the few students brave (or dumb) enough to show up for classes.

My first day of school

I "volunteered" to be the last one delivered because I enjoyed that horse-drawn sleigh ride.

4

Over the Wires and through the Snow

My dad and uncle rented a horse-drawn bobsled to take the two families to our grandparents' home. It was in Lewisville, Idaho, several miles west of Rigby.

Everyone piled in and covered themselves with blankets and quilts, trying to stay warm. It was a severe winter and driving a car even that short distance was impossible. No snow had been removed from the roads and strong, cold winds had created huge snowdrifts

We hadn't gone far when my uncle stopped the horses and told all the children to get out of the sled. My dad asked him why. My uncle replied, "Because it is an opportunity. There will probably never again be a situation where they'll be able to walk over telephone wires!"

The snow had indeed drifted that high with an icy crust created by the intense cold. We were able to walk over the telephone lines. Adults would have broken through the crust, but the children had no difficulty.

Have you ever walked over telephone lines?

Airplane in Town

♦

Soon after lunch one day, the elementary school principal announced classes were dismissed. There would be no more schooling that day because he thought it was more important for all of us to go to a nearby field and see the real airplane that had just landed!

Wow! It was like July 4th and Thanksgiving rolled into one.

Residents of Rigby and of neighboring towns converged on that field as word quickly spread. It was the first time most of us had ever seen a real airplane, except for an occasional small speck in the distant sky.

Upon reaching the airplane I actually went up and touched it! What a thrill! This large machine actually carried people through the air I was breathing! It went up to and through clouds!

Airplane in town! "Once around Rigby, only $5.00."

The pilot stood beside the airplane and said, "Ride in my airplane, once around the town. Only $5.00."

Few people in that large crowd of excited people had five dollars. And those who did weren't sure riding once around Rigby was worth that much money. Men who had jobs during those depression days were seldom paid more than two dollars for a hard day's work.

Regardless, that barnstorming pilot did alright. He assisted a paying passenger into his two-place aircraft, belted the excited person into the front open cockpit, and then climbed in, warning observers to "Stand back. Far back!" Those who hadn't obeyed his advice were quick to comply when he started his powerful engine and the propeller whirled faster and faster until it was a mere blur.

Upon releasing the brakes, the airplane moved toward the end of the pasture. Turning into the wind, the pilot applied full throttle and the plane soon picked up the speed necessary to take off.

Everyone watched in awe as the airplane climbed to perhaps five hundred feet or so. Then the pilot banked for a turn to circumnavigate Rigby. And it didn't take long. Gliding in for a smooth landing, the plane came to a stop and another paying passenger climbed into the forward cockpit for his ride.

As the sun was about to set and the plane departed, I went home to find my dad had been watching the flights too. He had taken a ride and looked for me so I could do the same. But he couldn't locate me in that large crowd. I was devastated. I so wanted to experience flight. It was a huge disappointment and I thought, "I missed the chance of a lifetime." I'm glad that wasn't so. I still love to fly (especially when I am at the controls).

Migrating Indians

◆

Every spring and every fall youngsters would run from house to house in Rigby, Idaho, shouting, "The Indians are coming! The Indians are coming!"

Indian woman with travois and dog

My mother, as most women, would prepare by wrapping up a loaf or two of homemade bread, and/or a bottle or two of home-canned fruit: apple sauce, pears, peaches, jellies, jams, etc.

When the Indians arrived at our front door, Mother would greet them (with my siblings and I close behind her) and give them her offering.

The Indians never said anything in English, nor did they even smile. With an uttered "ugh," they accepted what they were given, then proceeded on to the next home.

The Indians always had horses and dogs, but the men walked from home to home while the women were on horseback or walked alongside the travois (a long pole on each side of a horse, extending back 8 or 10 feet, with a blanket or animal hide connected to each pole, supporting their belongings.)

Train versus Tanker Truck

Our home in Rigby was on the south side of town, just two blocks west of the highway to Idaho Falls. There was a huge expanse of sage brush between the homes there and the rodeo grandstand.

One summer day, as I was mowing our lawn, a loud explosion shook the ground and a black plume of smoke arose from what I knew were the railroad tracks crossing the highway. The train had struck a gasoline tanker truck! Flames seemed to push the smoke upward as they pinpointed the location.

I climbed on my bicycle and was the first one on the scene.

The truck driver told me he hadn't seen the train and didn't know it had struck his gasoline tank trailer until he heard the explosion and saw the flames in his rear view mirror! His truck wasn't damaged. The tank was destroyed. The train engineer died—reportedly upon impact.

It was a terrible accident that resulted in an overpass being constructed to prevent a recurrence.

Fourth of July Stampede

There was a lot of excitement in Rigby as a well-advertised Fourth of July parade marched down Main Street. There was music, people waved flags, and youngsters fired off firecrackers.

I was in front of the town's auto repair shop, hanging onto a ledge that gave me a good view of the parade, looking over the heads of the crowd that lined the sidewalk.

An especially large firecracker (called a Cherry Bomb) exploded as a team of huge Clydesdale horses was passing. They stampeded and the crowd dispersed, yelling and screaming. The handler of the horses had no control. The frightened behemoths trampled and propelled the terrified onlookers, men, women and children.

One of the panicked horses rushed in my direction, nostrils flared and eyes wide. He ran into the garage door, crushing a man near me that was leaning against it.

I couldn't believe it was happening and I don't remember experiencing fear for my own safety as I saw the carnage—people crying, moaning, calling for help. It was a major tragedy and I was right in the middle of it, unhurt.

And no, I had no firecrackers.

Fishing Amid Rattlesnakes

◆

My dad was an expert fly fisherman. He caught trout, big ones, even when nobody else could. He tied his own fly hooks and knew just where and how to place them to entice fish. But, he hated the rattlesnakes that too often sounded off within striking distance. I was his rattlesnake guard. And I had quite a collection of rattles.

I didn't kill the snakes if it wasn't necessary. I often used my walking stick to fling them some safe distance away, or even into the river. But most of the time, I'd find them coiled at Dad's feet, head back, ready to strike when he moved. He didn't move. He'd call to me and I'd dispatch the snake so he could continue fishing.

I didn't kill the snakes if it wasn't necessary.

On one occasion, on a tiny island called "The Overflows" created by the Civilian Conservation Corps, Dad found perfect fly fishing, catching one large trout after another. But he called for me every few minutes. That island was home to many rattlers. I killed eight of them before Dad had his limit of trout.

The Snake River is not named after snakes. It is so named because of the way it winds through its course. Fishermen now seldom even see a snake.

Snake Show

♦

Rattlesnakes were not the only snakes I found while accompanying Dad on his fishing trips. There were blow snakes, water snakes, king snakes and other harmless varieties, some tiny and some large, up to five feet long.

One time, I brought a collection home. My siblings and I ran from house to house throughout our neighborhood to announce the opening of our "Snake Show." Admission was quite nominal. We only charged five safety pins, two or three rubber bands, two or three wooden clothespins (to use to make rubber band guns), etc.

"After the show, you may take one snake home with you."

As most of the kids living nearby assembled in our backyard, my two brothers and I ceremoniously dumped my bag full of snakes onto a tarpaulin. Then we each held up several snakes, draping some over our arms and around our necks.

It was harmless entertainment, until we let our guests take some home as gifts. Their parents were not all pleased!

Skiing and Arrowheads

Hills west of Rigby, called the Big Buttes, were a favorite recreation area for my brother and me.

In the summertime we searched under sagebrush for Indian arrowheads. It was undoubtedly an area where the Indians had battled because we found many arrowheads, varying in sizes and shapes.

On Saturdays in the winters, we skied down the hills. We even made ski jumps, piling and pounding the snow to increase speed and height.

The skis we used were about 4 inches wide, 8 feet long, weighed a lot and had only a single strap to hold them onto our overshoes! We'd cinch that strap as tightly as possible, but the skis often came off, sometimes in mid-flight as we flew off the ski jump. Turning was nearly impossible. But we had fun.

Indian Guests and Gold

♦

My grandparents Jardine had a home in the near center of Lewisville, with at least one full block of land. They always had a large garden, but most of the land was fallow.

Though many white people seemed to dislike the Indians, my grandparents always treated them well. Grandfather allowed Indian bands to put up their teepees and rest a few days as they made their semiannual treks north and south.

The leader of one band, requesting permission to stay on the Jardine grounds (and use their garden) told Grandfather they were hoping a young squaw could catch up to them before they had to move on. She had stayed behind to have a baby!

After a few days passed without any word from the new mother, the band had to resume their journey. The Indian leader again approached Grandfather and said, "We thank you for your kindnesses. Will you please tell squaw with papoose that we'll camp near the falls of the big water for five suns. She can join us there."

The band was headed for Idaho Falls, about 15 miles south of Lewisville. They planned to stay there for five days.

When the squaw appeared two days later, with a tiny papoose on her back, my grandparents were appalled by her condition. She was obviously tired, worn, hungry and yet concerned about catching up to her people.

Grandmother insisted the squaw and child stay for a day or so, to rest and better prepare for the resumption of their journey. She put them in a bed (almost unheard of in those days), fed the mother and cared for the two for two days.

As the squaw was insisting they must leave to catch up with their group, she thanked her hosts most profusely and handed a buckskin pouch to Grandfather. It contained several ounces of gold, mostly gold dust but also with some rather large nuggets.

Grandfather wanted, of course, to know where she had found the gold. The squaw provided "detailed information," but refused to retrace her journey to pinpoint the source of the gold.

Grandfather made several trips north of Lewisville to try and find the gold, unsuccessfully. And after his death, Grandmother spent a small fortune "grub-staking" men who had heard the story and wanted to search.

Someday, somebody will find the gold "three suns northwest, past the big hills, then nine suns north to the river that is lost. When the river forks, follow the waters on the east side until a tongue of small rocks reaches out into the river. There you will find the pretty yellow metal."

My father kept some of that gold in a small plastic pill bottle for years. I sometimes took it to school to show skeptical friends.

They were convinced. And if you look at a map of Idaho, there is a river in that area called Lost River!

The Butcher Shop

◆

There were many times, when I was a youngster, that Mother handed me a quarter, with instructions to go to the butcher shop and "buy 20 cents worth of round steak, tenderized, and 5 cents worth of liver."

The butcher weighed and tenderized the round steak (using a metal mallet with perhaps 30 pounding surfaces) while I ate free hotdogs and/or salted sardines he kept there for waiting customers.

With the steak packaged and ready to go, the butcher would always say, "Tell me when to stop cutting," as he held liver over his cutting board. Five cents would buy as much as you wanted, so liver and onions was on most residents' menus during the big depression of the thirties.

At the butcher's

Idaho Potatoes 5 Cents

During the great depression of the 1930's, there were few jobs available. The federal government offered some assistance with special job programs. Most were very humbling and all involved low pay for back-breaking eight-hour days, digging irrigation and sewer ditches with shovels and pick-axes for two dollars daily.

Some "surplus" food items were provided. Cornmeal was abundant. Housewives used it, and potatoes, to feed their families with an extremely wide variety of recipes, traded among friends and relatives.

Fortunately for us, we could often supplement our meals with fish. Dad was an expert fly fisherman and knew where and how to catch rainbow, German brown, brook, speckled and other trout.

Even so, the "spud cellar" located near the Rigby train station was the source of our main food supply. Every summer I'd take my wagon, an empty burlap bag and 5 cents to the spud cellar. Every winter I'd take my sled. I'd hand the burlap bag and nickel to the first worker I saw and he would place a hundred-pound bag of perfect Idaho potatoes on my wagon or sled.

We ate a lot of potatoes (boiled, fried, baked, stuffed, etc.) and people in Idaho know dozens of ways to prepare potatoes to eat.

Now, *one* potato costs far more than 5 cents!

Rigby Water Tower

♦

I liked the steel water tower in Rigby, Idaho. I've always enjoyed being up high, and that water tower was one of the tallest structures in town.

I'd climb to the *top* and enjoy the view at length.

Adults frequently called up to me, urging or ordering me to "Come down!"

They didn't come up after me!

On the water tower in Rigby, Idaho

Schools in Rigby

◆

Schools in Rigby, Idaho were enjoyable, and I had excellent teachers.

In second grade, we "learned" how to set a table, and proper table manners. (All of which my mother had already taught me.) It amazed me that many of my classmates were unaware of these things, but they certainly learned. The teacher believed it to be vitally important, not something to be ignored.

My third grade teacher was a frustrated high school English teacher. At least her training was to teach English. There were no English teaching positions open in our school district when she applied for a job, so, when she accepted a third grade teaching assignment, she taught high school English! It was one of my favorite classes and a familiar subject from then on. I attribute much of my success in future schooling to that third grade teacher.

I was in class at Rigby Junior High School when the high school principal sent for me. Inexplicably, I had gained a reputation for being good at art, and he wanted me to illustrate the high school yearbook!

I did. However, what it really amounted to was copying the principal's drawings and cartoons. He was a frustrated artist!

Rigby High School was on a lyceum circuit. We had some awesome assemblies.

Jim Thorpe, the Oklahoma Indian All-American football player was the subject for one memorable assembly. He came on stage dressed in full Indian regalia: war bonnet trailing to the floor, buckskins with long fringes, moccasins and the beat of an Indian drum. He danced around the stage with dramatic whoops and hollers while students gazed in awe. Then he shared his football experiences. A choice assembly!

The most impressive and memorable assembly featured Glenn Cunningham, who at one time held the world record for the mile run.

Glenn told how he and his older brother Floyd, attending their local one-room school, were taking their turn building a fire to warm the room before classes began.

Jim Thorpe dancing at Rigby High School lyceum

Glenn's brother got the fire started in a stove in the room's center. Then, to hasten the heat, he poured what he thought to be kerosene on the flames. But it wasn't kerosene. The can had been filled with gasoline!

Flames exploded and both boys were burned, Floyd fatally. Glenn's burns were severe. Doctors said he'd never walk again.

That was unacceptable to Glenn's mother. Every night she massaged his burned legs for long periods of time.

Glenn described dragging himself through the school's door at recess. He braced himself against the outside wall and inched upward until he was standing. Fellow students, running around the building, weren't too careful. One of them knocked Glenn over. As he fell, he felt his hip twist, thereby swinging one leg forward. He pivoted on that leg as he fell to the ground. He had taken a step! He was overjoyed! Thereafter, he often inched himself up a wall, then deliberately fell forward. But he'd swing a leg ahead so he could experience the same wonderful pivoting movement.

Eventually, he was able to swing a leg, pivot, swing the other leg, pivot, and go increasingly forward. That led to his ability to run! His determination led to him falling repeatedly, but he was thrilled that he was making excellent progress. Though unable, initially, to walk, Glenn was able to run. He built his stamina and it eventually led him to his running Olympics, and to setting a world record, close to a four-minute mile.

Glenn's successes prompted me to learn a quotation by an author that was unknown to me before writing this book, but now revealed by the miracle of the Internet as composer and librettist Gian Carlo Menotti:

> Hell begins on the day God grants us a clear vision of all we might have achieved, of all the gifts we have wasted, of all we might have done but did not do.

I believe *determination* is the key to success, and Glenn Cunningham is a good example.

Trapping and Hockey on the Canals

◆

The Great Depression of the 1930's was having a negative effect upon every family in Rigby, Idaho. With seven of us in my family and very little income, I, as the oldest child, did my best to help out, though I was a pre-teen.

On one visit to my grandparents Jardine in Lewisville, I noticed more than a dozen old iron traps hanging by their chains. Upon inquiry, I learned my dad and his four brothers had once trapped muskrats and weasels to earn "spending money." But the traps had not been used for several years. Grandfather Jardine told me I could have the traps—if I'd use them.

I took the rusty traps home, used steel wool and oil to renew them, then followed instructions regarding what to use as bait, where and how to set them for maximum effectiveness, and started my new enterprise. Successfully!

The weather was cold and snow drifts made it difficult for me to carry those traps to a large, ice-covered canal nearly a mile from my home.

Weasels had changed from summer brown to brilliant white (in which state they are called ermines). And there was a good market for them. Had I publicized my trapping venture, I'm sure many others would have competed with me. Knowing that, I kept my new business secret.

Running a line of fifteen or sixteen traps was a daily effort. If I had missed a day, predators would have feasted on my fur bearing animals. The income from my trapping proved to be a God-send for my family.

Trapping animals was not the only enticement to visit the ice-covered canals near Rigby. We swam, skated, trapped, and fished on Rigby's canals.

Friends joined my brother and me there on cold winter days whenever we could take the time. We formed ice skating clubs, playing hockey with branches from trees for hockey sticks and flattened evaporated milk cans for pucks.

Our ice skates were truly primitive too. They were "clamp-ons," which fastened onto our shoes by tightening screws with a special key. Sometimes our very active play exerted too much stress and the sole of a shoe separated. Then we'd take the shoe to the local shoemaker where the sole could be nailed and sewn back in place. For a price. That was expensive—but necessary.

Most young people had only one pair of shoes (and one pair of rubbers or overshoes). When we went to church, we'd polish our shoes "for dress." Those same shoes were worn for work in potato fields, for thinning and topping sugar beets, fishing, trapping, hunting, and school. We "saved" our shoes by going barefoot during summer months.

Severe austerity ruled.

Young Driver

♦

Practically all my school friends lived on farms near Rigby. The boys were experienced drivers of tractors and other farm machinery. Most of them even drove their family's automobile and truck at an early age.

I felt deprived because I lived in town and we had only the family car. Nevertheless, Dad taught me how to start it, depress the clutch, shift gears, and steer it before I was twelve years old.

Dad fishing on the Snake River

Dad enjoyed the good fly fishing near our home in Rigby and the family enjoyed the trout. But like any good fly fisherman, Dad moved along the streams and rivers as he continuously cast artificial fly hooks to entice the fish.

There was usually a bridge across the fishing waters approximately every mile. Dad fished downstream from one bridge to the next while I drove the car, parking and waiting for him at each successive bridge.

It was a convenience for Dad and good experience for me.

Attacked by a Golden Eagle

◆

It was a crispy cold, but sunny, late fall day as my dad and his brother Cec fished along the Snake River in Idaho. I was hunting cottontail rabbits with a small .410 shotgun, wading through sixteen inches of snow in my ten inch high overshoes.

A large shadow passed over me, moving rapidly. Looking up, I saw a golden eagle climbing high overhead. Suddenly, with an ear-splitting shriek, it whirled into a steep dive coming directly at me with talons extended!

Reacting with my only defense, I raised my shotgun and fired at the attacking bird. Tiny pellets from that shell struck the eagle in his chest, resulting in a shower of pin feathers. And he swerved from his dive, shrieking loudly. But he was not hurt.

Three more times the eagle climbed, then dove at me. I fired at him each time, finally realizing that he was after the two cottontail rabbits I had hanging from my belt. He was after a rabbit dinner, but I wanted one too.

With only three or four shotgun shells remaining, I fired from a greater distance. That created a wider dispersal of BB's from the .410 shell, as I knew it would. Although I did not want to hurt that magnificent bird, I was truly desperate.

The pellets from my last shot apparently hit the eagle in his face. He shrieked like a banshee and flew away as my dad and uncle reached me, running from different directions.

I'm glad they saw that huge bird because, if they hadn't, I doubt they would have believed my story detailing his size and fierce attack.

A golden eagle is often larger than the well-known bald eagle, our national bird. In fact, research reveals that adult male golden eagles weigh on average about 7 ½ pounds and females 11 pounds, with typical wing spans of 7 ½ feet.

I was twelve years old.

Years later, while driving through Wyoming, I saw a golden eagle standing in a field next to the highway. He appeared to be no less than three feet tall!

Aerial Balloonist

The residents of Rigby, Idaho were excited about a coming event scheduled to open the annual three-day rodeo. Bareback and saddle bronc riding, racing, steer wrestling, calf roping, and wild bull riding were always exciting and fun to watch, especially when several young men in town were participating. However, this year something unique had been added.

There was a colorful, dramatic poster on every telephone pole and many trees throughout the town. And people were talking about them.

Just prior to the first rodeo event, a hot air balloon was going to take its owner and his dog to a height of at least five hundred feet. Then the dog would leave the balloon and descend by parachute!

My brother Max and I were among the dozens of onlookers that fateful day.

A 50 gallon steel drum was rolled into the basket beneath the huge, tethered, multi-colored balloon and filled with an inflammable. Then the balloonist called for spectators to hold the balloon while he lit the drum afire. The balloon would thereby be filled with the hot air necessary to ascend, carrying the balloonist and his dog to the widely advertised five hundred feet or so.

All the volunteers surrounding the balloon rushed forward, grabbed a section of the huge balloon and gripped tightly per instructions. We were all looking forward to seeing the dog descend safely from such a high place.

Unfortunately, there was a strong wind blowing. Everyone struggled to keep that beautiful silk balloon from getting dangerously close to flames which were now leaping up four to six feet above the steel drum. We weren't successful.

Even with men holding desperately onto every available inch of the balloon's circumference, it was impossible to keep it from the flames. It had only begun to inflate when it caught fire and was quickly reduced to ashes.

There was no balloon ascent or parachute jump that year.

The balloonist sat on the ground near the smoldering remains of his source of livelihood—and cried.

There was no balloon ascent that year.

Ram Attack

◆

The Big Buttes Bridge that spans Idaho's Snake River was less than 100 yards west of me as I fished from the south bank.

A horrendous odor began to assail my nostrils. As it grew steadily worse I looked around for the source.

Coming across the bridge toward me was a huge wild ram with dirty, shaggy wool hanging all the way to the ground.

It kept coming...off the bridge and toward me.

As it got closer, the stench was almost unbearable. Much worse than a skunk! I must have thrown a rock or two to motivate that disgusting animal to change direction.

The stinky ram

Wrong motivation!

He lowered his huge, curved horns and charged me at a gallop.

I dropped my fishing pole and ran to a nearby tree. Its four-inch trunk didn't provide much protection, but I felt safer as long as I kept it between me and the angry ram.

Believe me, that beast was determined to do me harm. As I ran around that small tree trunk he attacked continuously, running almost as fast as I was.

During the entire attack I was shouting for help from Dad and my Uncle Cec. Cec heard me and came as fast as he could, wondering why I was yelling. He certainly recognized that I was desperate, in deep trouble.

Before Cec reached me, I was so exhausted from trying to avoid being gored, I finally took a stance. I turned, grabbed the ram by his horns, twisted his neck and fell on him. He went down but he struggled very strongly to regain his feet.

When Uncle Cec arrived and saw my predicament, he laughed. I told him how difficult it was to bulldog the ram and he sneered! He was a rodeo performer; he didn't believe it could be that hard. I released the ram and jumped behind the tree. The ram jumped up, Cec grabbed him, but could not get him back down. The ram kept attacking.

Cec ran to the car while I remained behind the tree trunk, got an ax and hit the ram between the eyes with the back of the ax. The ram was stunned, but even then Cec couldn't throw him down.

I'm sure my adrenalin was 100% active—but it was a frightening and memorable experience. My mother agreed. She said she could smell the odor as our car approached the house, from a full block away!

I believe she burned my clothes.

Bouncing Ball Lightning

♦

My brother Max and I were riding our bicycles at top speed. We were heading for home in Rigby, hoping to arrive before the onslaught of a thunderstorm racing toward us.

As we flew down the highway about eight or ten feet apart, I sensed a light behind us. Turning to look, I saw a large ball of light overtaking us. It was *bouncing* along the highway. I called to Max and he watched it with me as it passed between, then ahead of us. The ball disappeared after proceeding a few hundred yards ahead.

When we later described this to adults, they said we had witnessed a very rare sight—ball lightning. And neither of us ever saw it again.

That ball of lightning appeared to be nearly twice the size of a basketball and it was really moving.

P.S. The storm beat us home. We got soaked minutes before reaching the door.

Big Black Stallion

◆

Keith Jenkins had a large farm just west of Rigby, Idaho. He also had two sons, Ferrin and Vaughn. Ferrin was my age, Vaughn, the same age as my younger brother Max.

When school was recessed each fall for potato and sugar beet harvesting, Mr. Jenkins hired Max and me. It was very hard work, from daylight to dark, but we earned good pay—and became closer friends with the Jenkins boys.

One summer day, Ferrin rode up to our home in Rigby. He was astride a huge black stallion, riding bareback.

He suggested that Max and I might like to ride his horse, one at a time.

Max, being much smarter than I, declined.

Ferrin demonstrated how he mounted and dismounted that *big* stallion by grabbing hold of its mane and swinging up or down.

I suggested he place the horse alongside the elevated front porch of my home so I could more readily position myself for the leisurely ride I was anticipating.

So much for anticipation!

As soon as I was astride that huge animal, he took off as though he was determined to place first in some important race. I wrapped my arms as far around his neck as possible and desperately clung to him for dear life. That animal was unlike any of the few docile ponies I'd previously ridden.

And I wasn't really "riding" the stallion. He was taking me for a ride! I was bouncing high above the horse, trying to stay aboard. (Falling was a long way down!)

The stallion ran through my mother's prized garden in our back yard, past the new WPA-built outhouse and under the clothesline wires.

The horse went under the wires; I didn't.

One of the wires strung to my forehead as the horse and I parted company—but only after the wire had stretched to its limit. Then I found out what an arrow feels like when fired from a powerful bow! I flew through the air what felt like thirty or forty feet in the opposite direction!

It required three or four stitches to repair the indentation left by that wire. I still have the scar—and I don't ride horses.

The horse went under the clothesline. I didn't! The wire became the bowstring. I was the arrow.

High School Luck

♦

I suppose we all have had periods of luck, real lucky streaks. One of mine began as junior high school ended. It surprised a lot of people, including me.

As a teenager I was somewhat bashful around girls. However, when a dance was added to the junior high school graduation schedule, I mustered up sufficient courage to invite gorgeous Mary George to be my date, and she accepted. Mary was a beautiful brunette with truly memorable eyes, a quick wit and a great personality. It was a fun date

In Rigby's high school the Junior Prom was a highlight of each year. I don't know how I got up the courage to ask Ada Gean Madsen, one of the most popular girls in our school, to be my prom date—but I did, and she accepted!

Ada Gean, a blue-eyed blonde, was a stand-out beauty everyone liked and admired. Her acceptance was an unexpected but pleasant surprise because I knew she was always besieged for dates. But that surprise was miniscule when compared to the one I experienced during intermission at the prom.

Surreptitiously, I had found out the color of my date's prom dress, ordered an appropriate corsage, scheduled and washed the family car, got a haircut, and shined my shoes. I was prepared for the prom.

Well—almost.

The dance was equal to my highest expectations—until a drum roll temporarily ended the music for intermission and attracted everyone's attention to the stage. Our school principal stood there, holding a microphone, obviously about to make an announcement.

When conversations ended and silence settled over the ballroom, a commanding voice shook me to the core.

"Will Ada Gean Madsen, our newly elected Queen for this year's Junior Prom, please come forward to accept her crown and give a brief acceptance speech?"

Ada Gean had been informed about her selection as Queen well in advance but had promised to keep her new royalty status secret until it was formally disclosed at the dance.

She made a beautiful Queen as I moved to the back of the ballroom, in the shadows.

The high school's next big occasion was the annual Senior Ball. Riding on my junior high school graduation and Junior Prom successes, I approached lovely Reva Hill to be my date for the Senior Ball.

I'd had quite a "crush" on Reva for a long time, but I lived in Rigby while she and a male friend lived on adjoining farms miles out of town. Inconvenient for me; good, for him.

Reva was a sparkling attraction in any crowd. She had a charming personality, an unforgettable smile, intelligence, heart-stopping beauty...and a boyfriend.

Nevertheless, she said yes to my invitation!

At the ball I was dancing on a cloud as the music ended for intermission.

It was readily acceptable to everyone when my date, Reva Hill, was introduced as Queen of the Senior Ball. A spotlight was on her as she proceeded to the stage to receive her crown. Like

37

Ada Gean, Reva had promised to keep her selection secret until it was revealed at the ball.

I beamed with pride and pleasure as Reva received her crown and scepter amid the applause of her subjects.

I pleasantly recalled these three dates—my exceptionally lucky streak—many times while fighting Japanese on Saipan and Tinian. And the memory of those dates remains after more than seventy years.

Thank you Mary, Reva, and Ada Gean.

A word of advice my mother always told me:

"Treat each girl you date as you would have other young men treat your sisters."

The girls and their parents will appreciate that.

Shot during a Pheasant Hunt

My younger brother Max and I were walking slowly through a field of sagebrush near our home in Rigby. I had my .22 rifle; Max was an observer.

.22 cartridges at that time cost about 18 cents for a box of 50 longs. They were far less expensive than shotgun shells, but also less productive.

I have never shot a pheasant on the ground and using a rifle bullet to hit a pheasant in flight suggests I was an expert shot. I did alright, but only because five or six birds were often flushed together. Hitting one of them was part marksmanship but mostly luck. I was quite lucky.

Suddenly I had a sharp pain in my left ear. I thought I'd been stung by a bee or hornet, but as I touched that ear my hand came away covered with blood. An unseen hunter in the vicinity was using a .22 rifle also, and he had put a bullet through the outer edge of my ear. Only inches away from my eye!

As Max and I headed for home, I told him not to say anything. I didn't want to be restricted from hunting due to someone else's carelessness.

Walking up to our house, bleeding profusely, I was hurrying to staunch the flow of blood and clean up before our mother saw me. No such luck! Max, ignoring my admonition, ran ahead shouting, "Mom, Don's been shot!"

It would not be the last time I was shot at.

DURING WORLD WAR II

December 7, 1941—Pearl Harbor Bombed

♦

Dad and I were in our family car, listening to the radio, when we heard the shocking news that Japanese aircraft were attacking Pearl Harbor! Few people in our town of Rigby, Idaho had even heard of Pearl Harbor or had any idea where it was located. But its proximity to Honolulu pinpointed it for us.

The entire United States was in shock. And angry!

According to media reports the following day, men intent upon enlisting in our Armed Forces lined up at every recruiting office in the nation.

We were all incensed at the audacity and deceit of the Japanese for conducting such a sneaky, dastardly aggression.

I was fifteen years old at the time, too young to be accepted by the military. Had I been older, I would have been among the first in line at an air force recruiting office. I had always aspired to be a pilot.

Within a few months it seemed all the eligible men in Rigby, including all members of the National Guard, were gone. The latter, including several of my uncles, were sent overseas quite rapidly. Men without military experience were in accelerated training programs and would soon be in war zones.

Move To Ogden

◆

Before school began that next September, my friend Dick Lessey, with whom I had attended school since kindergarten, moved to Ogden, Utah. The senior high school there had an R.O.T.C. (Reserve Officers' Training Corps) program. Dick urged me to join him.

There wasn't any work for my dad and his friends in Rigby, so they sought and found employment in Ogden where there were job opportunities galore. That meant forming car pools, driving from Rigby to Ogden every Sunday evening, working through the week, then returning to Rigby late Friday afternoons for another short weekend.

Moving families was not possible for a variety of reasons: children in schools, church assignments, affiliations—but the main reason was housing. There wasn't a house available in or near Ogden for sale or rent. Workers converged on Ogden from hundreds of miles in every direction for employment in "war work" at Second Street, The Arsenal, Hill Air Force Base, and other facilities.

Dad had a sleeping room in the Oak Hotel, just off notorious (at the time) 25th street in downtown Ogden.

After considerable pleading, my parents agreed I could move to Ogden, stay with dad, and enroll in Ogden Senior High School *if* I paid my own way, all expenses: school fees and supplies, transportation, clothing, medical and dental bills, meals, and half the hotel bill. I agreed, knowing I'd be working and studying every weekend, unable to accompany Dad to our home in Idaho.

After signing up for high school classes, including R.O.T.C., I was advised to obtain employment at UAQSD (the Utah Army Quartermaster Supply Depot) commonly called "Second Street." It was a huge facility with military supplies stored in many giant warehouses.

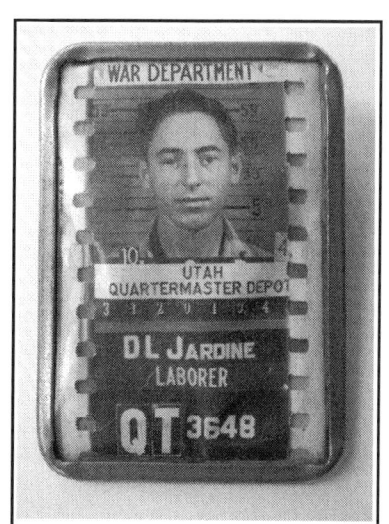

ID badge for Utah Quartermaster Supply Depot

I really "lucked out." I applied for employment and was placed in charge of the base message center on the eight-hour evening shift.

A special bus took all UAQSD employees from the high school to our jobs immediately after the last class each day. We worked from 3:30 p.m. until 12 midnight with half an hour off for a paper bag "dinner."

All the messengers were cute high school girls, some my classmates! It was a rough job but someone had to do it.

When an important order arrived from a combat area, it was "redlined" and rushed to the appropriate warehouse or warehouses via messenger on a motor scooter. We had twelve of those vehicles, each capable of speeds up to thirty-five miles per hour.

Many Italian prisoners of war were barracked and worked at Second Street. Truckloads of them were transported around the base as needed. And you've never seen happier men in your life! They were out of the war, safe, in comfortable accommodations, enjoying regular meals and were just waiting for the war to end so they could return to their homes in Italy.

They had beautiful voices and sang happy songs wherever they went. They smiled, waved and called us friends—especially the girl messengers on their motor scooters.

A New House at Sixteen!

When government housing, a new development in South Ogden, became available, I applied for a house! Housing authorities objected, saying I was too young to qualify for a house. But when I pointed out that regulations didn't specify a minimum age for applicants and I proved I was a full time department head in a major government facility engaged in war work, I became the proud tenant of I-14 Army Way, Washington Terrace, Ogden, Utah.

My mother, two brothers and two sisters could now join Dad and me in Ogden.

The three-bedroom unit was small compared to our home in Rigby, but we were together. Dad and I were happy to leave the hotel and he was spared the long round trip drive to Rigby every weekend.

I was the family hero and I was sixteen years old.

New Job

◆

After working at UAQSD for a year, I learned about an employment opportunity at nearby Hill Air Force Base that paid a substantially higher salary. I applied for and got the job. It was with the Area Engineers, working as a rod-and-chain man for a team of surveyors.

As the new man on the job, I was often given the task of going for supplies, delivering reports, picking up lunches ordered by phone, and other menial assignments all over that large base.

My boss decided I needed a military driver's license and arranged for me to take the required tests. I passed. I was surprised that the list of vehicles I was authorized to drive included light and medium tanks!

One could easily imagine a light tank would have probably been a more appropriate vehicle than the dump truck I was told to use for a special errand. That huge truck was the only vehicle available, and I had never before driven anything that large.

Don Jardine ID at Hill Air Force Base

I'm quite sure the entire survey crew watched as I started the engine and spent at least five minutes getting it into the correct forward gear.

If that amused them, and I'm sure it did, imagine the hilarity they would have experienced had they seen me try to back out of the parking lot at my destination.

I had parked near the lot's exit, anticipating a possible problem if I had to back out of a parking space. That problem became a reality when someone parked in front of the dump truck, effectively preventing me from just pulling forward.

That truck didn't seem to have a reverse gear. I thought I'd tried everything, but every gear just moved the truck forward. One thing for sure—it was properly named a dump truck. I was mortified when I accidentally activated the dump! Then I couldn't get it down!

I did finally get the truck into reverse, but I had to return to our office with the dump bed *up*, to the amusement of my fellow workers.

While with the Area Engineers, the front window in our office looked out upon a main runway. We often watched the planes land, including large bombers. As a plane's wheels touched down, there was an inevitable screeching of the tires, obviously wasting precious rubber. Many large planes had multiple tires and made numerous landings every day.

Civilians had difficulty buying tires to replace worn out automobile tires because they were strictly rationed. And the tires on a civilian's car were almost insignificant compared to the large, special tires on military aircraft.

One of the engineers decided to resolve the problem. His solution was remarkably simple. He designed half-moon "cups" on the outer edge of each wheel. Military aircraft usually lowered their landing gear on approach to a runway at speeds in excess of one-hundred miles per hour. The "cups" caught the resulting wind-stream, causing the wheels to rotate. Having the wheels moving at touchdown dramatically reduced the wear on rubber tires.

The engineer reportedly received a nice check from Uncle Sam when his solution was adopted. It prolonged the useful life of countless aircraft tires at a time when rubber was a scarce and important commodity.

Hungry for my First Flight

♦

I have always been fascinated by flying.

While a student at Utah's Ogden Senior High School, my friend Cappy Ricks and I went without lunches for most of a school year saving the lunch money to pay for our first flight.

The big day finally arrived, sunny and calm. Cappy and I drove to Ogden Air Park, hurried into the pilots' lounge and introduced ourselves to the man who would take us off the ground, into and above the clouds.

As we each paid our half of the flight charges, Cappy asked about parachutes. Our pilot laughed and said they'd be aboard. "But you won't need them, I guarantee!"

We climbed aboard a high wing, five passenger WACO cabin plane, fastened our seat belts and adjusted radio headsets. Then the pilot started the engine, checked his instruments, released the brakes, and we taxied down to the far end of the runway.

With the landing pattern clear of approaching planes, we turned into the wind and rapidly accelerated down the long runway, picking up the speed necessary for take-off. Hangars and parked cars flew rapidly by our windows as the WACO smoothly lifted off the runway, airborne!

What an exhilarating sensation!

Our pilot banked out of the flight pattern and headed toward Great Salt Lake. It was far bigger from this vantage point than I had imagined. It looked like an ocean.

Crossing over Antelope Island, we saw the large herd of bison we had been advised to watch for. Then our pilot asked what we'd like to do, where we wanted to go. I'm sure he was somewhat surprised when we asked him to climb above the fluffy looking small white clouds, then dive and loop the plane.

No way. But he did take us above and through two small cumulus clouds, then we flew over Salt Lake City and Ogden before our ride terminated. It had been a great flight—exceeding our expectations. We were hooked. We both aspired to become pilots.

The Royal Canadian Air Force

◆

High school graduation, mid-school-year, was imminent. World War II was being waged over most of the globe. Friends were receiving their draft notices and would soon be leaving for basic training, most of them in the army or navy.

My friend Cappy and I had other plans. We wanted to fly.

The recruiting office for the U.S. Air Corps was crowded with young men as we entered.

Most of those ahead of us left very soon after short conversations with recruiters. We were no exception. We quickly learned that enlistments in the U.S. Air Corps (later Air Force) were not open to anyone under eighteen years of age. Cappy and I were seventeen.

I was not deterred. The Royal Canadian Air Force (RCAF) was accepting enlistees at age seventeen. My mother was born in Canada and I had relatives there. My problem was solved!

Not quite.

After applying for enlistment in the RCAF, I was informed that the U.S. Congress had just passed a law prohibiting the enlistment of U.S. citizens in the armed forces of a foreign country while the U.S. itself is at war. That is why American pilots in Canada's RCAF, in Britain's Royal Air Force (the Eagle Squadron), and in China's AVG (American Volunteer Group—Chenault's Flying Tigers) were required to transfer into the United States Air Force.

Canada gave me the option of enlistment but with the proviso of losing American citizenship.

That was why I enlisted, at seventeen, in the United States Marine Corps. Citizenship in the United States of America was even more important to me than flying.

Enlistment—U.S. Marine Corps

When my parents agreed to sign for my underage enlistment in the Marine Corps, the recruiter promised, "Your son won't go overseas until he is 18, and he will get a thirty-day furlough before he boards any ship."

Wrong.

During my entire time in the Marine Corps, I was allowed no more than two or three forty-eight-hour passes and a few twenty-four hour passes (all in California) and perhaps six twelve-hour passes!

I was wounded the first time just 21 days after my 18th birthday, and I had already been overseas nearly four months. Actually, I received my honorable discharge from the Marine Corps at age nineteen—while still a teenager!

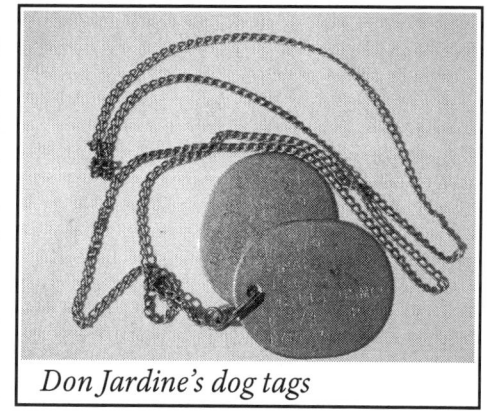

Don Jardine's dog tags

Years later, after I married, I learned that my new brother-in-law had also served in the Marine Corps, as did his wife. When my oldest son was of age, he too enlisted in the United States Marine Corps.

Boot Camp

◆

The railroad station in Ogden, Utah probably replicated a scene at every train depot in America. Young men were boarding transportation to their military training destinations, and families, friends, and neighbors were seeing them off.

Some for the last time.

As the conductor called out "All aboard!" the train's loud whistle attacked our ears with an urgency that let us all know the train was about to move.

Sobbing mothers and sisters were kissing and hugging their sons and brothers; dads and younger brothers were shaking their sons' and brothers' hands; wives and girlfriends were weeping and clinging to their husbands and boyfriends; and it seemed everyone was clicking the shutter of their Kodak Brownie camera. Then we hurriedly boarded the train.

The train was a Pullman. We would be sleeping on the train that night.

Most of us, future Marines and sailors en route to our respective boot camps, were headed for San Diego. Others were going to Army forts or Air Corps bases.

Waving as long as our loved ones could be seen, we then settled down for a very long train ride.

The train continued picking up more men along the way, so that before we reached San Diego, it was overloaded, packed with humanity. Men exited from every door as the train slowed to a stop at the final depot.

Waiting buses filled rapidly and headed to their respective destinations.

As my bus arrived at RDMCB (Recruit Depot, Marine Corps Base), we future Marines were greeted by a salty Master Gunnery Sergeant who used words I had never heard before—but would soon become well acquainted with.

Recruits counted off until the number required for a platoon was reached. Then a very mean-looking, authoritative Drill Instructor (D.I.) took immediate charge of *his* platoon, using many of the words we had so recently been greeted with. Very intimidating.

I was among the group that became Platoon #85, Corporal Smalley's platoon.

After forming *his* recruits into four ranks and calling us to "Attention!" the Corporal stood, feet apart and hands on his hips, looking at us for a few minutes. Then, with a look of utter disgust, he announced that we were the sorriest looking group he had ever seen. "But that will soon change," he promised (or threatened!).

Moving along the ranks, standing before each man in turn, the D.I. heard every one give his full name and hometown, as ordered.

When he stood in front of one tall, muscular man, he heard, "J. P. Morgan, Bushyhead, Oklahoma, sir."

Because we were all under orders to give our *full* name, Corporal Smalley shouted, "Repeat!"

"J. P. Morgan, Bushyhead, Oklahoma, sir!"

As the Corporal's face turned red with anger, he again said, "Repeat!" and received the same reply.

Then, before exploding, a light must have turned on. The Corporal grabbed the man's identification tag and read, "J. P. Morgan. Bushyhead, Oklahoma."

The muscular recruit had been adopted as a babe by a Morgan family. They decided to call him by the initials "J. P.", so it *was* his full name (and, at age 22, he had been mayor of that small town in Oklahoma).

Our platoon was not getting off to a very good start.

Upon receiving the record of every man in his new platoon, Corporal Smalley (a Marine who had served in China and who had been 18 years in the Corps) assigned me to be Right Guide for the platoon, based upon my two years of senior high school Reserve Officers Training Corps (ROTC).

Every boot camp or basic training camp, regardless of the branch of military, is identical in one objective. Every trainee is taught to accept *strict discipline.* It is also probable that each one is humbled in a similar way, a *shaved head.*

Some among us had shoulder length hair. I thought they'd shed tears as base barbers sheared their locks.

"Sir" became the most commonly used word by all of us, regardless of the person being addressed. After all, we were the lowest of the low.

We quickly filed past clerks who issued our uniforms faster than we could be measured.

Depositing our new attire on assigned bunks, we then marched double-time to a supply building where we were handed an M1 Garand rifle, steel helmet, cartridge belt (without ammo), a canteen, compass, K-bar knife with sheath, a bayonet, first aid kit, etc.

Taps was played quite early. *Lights out!*

Reveille was also played early. Very early. It was still dark. Certainly somebody had made a serious error.

We were given a few minutes to shower, shave, dress, make up our bunks, grab our mess kits, and form ranks for roll call. *Don't be late.* Then we were hurried off to the mess hall for breakfast. *Hurry! Hurry! Yes SIR! Hurry! Yes SIR! Hurry! Hurry!*

We learned to dress "properly," make up our bunk per regulations, clean our immediate surroundings, and march, march, march!

The D.I. demonstrated disassembling then reassembling our rifle, blindfolded. We were expected to do the same, first without blindfolds, then with blindfolds. That required intense concentration and accuracy. (There was a time limit.)

Again in formation, Corporal Smalley twisted his face into a threatening mask, looked at each of us (including large, athletic, muscular men you wouldn't want to tangle with) then said, "You don't love me now nor will you ever show me affection, but you have no idea right now of the hell I am going to put you through. I promise! So, I'm now giving you one chance to dance! If anyone wants to take me on, let's do it *right now*, or put it out of your mind completely!"

"Do I have any takers?"

There were none.

Training was intense. Marines fighting the Japanese in the jungles of South Pacific islands needed replacements, and all the help they could get, as soon as possible.

Nobody got the leave we had been promised following the ninety days of Boot Camp. Instead, we were transported to Camp Pendleton for advanced training.

Camp Pendleton

◆

At Camp Pendleton, we learned hand-to-hand combat, use of bayonets and knives, throwing live hand grenades, and more, followed by extensive training on the rifle range.

We ran, hiked, broke our own blisters, then ran some more.

The obstacle course was dreaded, and rightfully so: jumping, climbing, squeezing beneath barbed wire, often in mud and water with live machine gun rounds being fired a few inches above our earth-hugging bodies, and nearby explosions set off by remote control. Not all were successful in completing it. They were issued medical discharges after it was definitely determined they weren't faking it to get a release from military service.

Swimming tests were difficult for many, but if they failed, rather than being discharged they could be held back to acquire the minimal swimming skills required of every Marine.

I thought the swimming was fun!

During our advanced training, we were actually offered some choices: special training in artillery, mortars, machine guns, tanks, flame throwers, radio, etc. Volunteers also were accepted for service in Alaska. We had not known that there was any Jap offensive that far north.

A large majority preferred going to the Southwest Pacific theater.

For me, it was a no-brainer. I dislike the cold.

Like most Marines in my units, I'd head for Los Angeles when I was fortunate enough to get a twenty-four or forty-eight hour pass.

My dad's brother, Uncle John "Jack" Jardine lived there—so I'd go to 520 South Serrano (just North of Wilshire Boulevard in West Los Angeles.) Jack had a nice apartment and lived alone, so I had a place to stay and a willing guide to the sights of the big city.

Jack took me to church (where I met some famous Hollywood people), and to Olvera Street (Mexican community), the Farmer's Market, Chinatown, the Walk of Stars near Grauman's Chinese Theater (very famous at the time), and to the famous Brown Derby restaurant (which *looked* like a brown derby;) where the stars dined.

The one twenty-four hour pass when Jack didn't have time for me, I went to Los Angeles with about ten or twelve buddies. When several decided to go to a burlesque theater, the four or five of us that couldn't (we were underage) waited for them in a nearby bookstore. No—not "adult." And two or more hours in a bookstore at that time seemed like a hundred!

Hawaiian Tattoos

We shipped out of San Diego in a rapid flurry of activity and were taken to Pearl Harbor, Hawaii. The Marine Corps base was quite nearby. That is where we stayed and stood inspections, exercised and trained. The first Saturday, we were all given passes from noon until 6:00 p.m. Buses took us to Honolulu, where we rushed to make the most of our six hours of freedom.

Tattoo parlors were kept busy. It seemed every Marine wanted at least one tattoo: USMC with globe and anchor, a black panther clawing his way up an arm, with bloody claws; hula girls in grass skirts; etc. By Monday morning, some of the newly decorated Marines were reporting to sick bay with badly infected arms.

Doctors reported the situation to our commanding officer and he ordered the entire contingent onto the parade ground. In loud and very plain terms the commanding officer furiously denounced tattoos and threatened to keep every Marine on base if even one more tattoo infection showed up at sick bay. He said we had an obligation to Marines in combat areas to arrive in top physical condition, ready to replace those who had been killed or wounded.

I was pleased that I had no tattoo.

Tokyo Rose

After one week in Oahu, we boarded a ship to nearby Kahului, Maui. Offloading from the ship onto Kahului's new pier, we boarded trucks that took us to a remote mountain camp where we were assigned to tents.

As soon as we were settled, we began to build a snap-shooting course for Marines training to be Browning Automatic Riflemen. I was one of them.

Our new camp was beautifully situated. A large canyon on the north boundary was festooned with colorful wild orchids, and we had a fantastic view of the ocean with many palm trees silhouetted against the Pacific.

I still recall the unmatchable nighttime beauty of a silver rainbow created by a full moon and moisture from a receding rainfall. The palm trees were black against the silver background and nobody could view it without a sense of awe.

None of us got any leaves on Maui. We weren't there long enough. The firing course was not quite completed when we received unexpected orders to pack up. We prepared our tents for protection from wind and rain over an extended period of time. Then we loaded our combat gear aboard trucks, and were transported back to the pier at Kahului, to board another ship. We were headed for combat.

Wrong.

We were never told our destination, even after we boarded the ship. We waited aboard for many hours and wondered why the ship was still tied to the pier. Why weren't we moving?

Finally, we were told we were returning to our camp! The same day we boarded ship, we were returned to the tents we had just secured for a long absence.

Tokyo Rose, an English-speaking Japanese radio personality, had broadcast the name of our unit, the name of the ship we had boarded, and...our destination! She also promised that our ship would soon encounter Japanese submarines that were awaiting our departure with torpedoes ready to make sure we would not reach Eniwetok safely!

That announcement shocked our officers and kept us in port.

The next morning, the decision was made to proceed. So we secured the tents again, boarded trucks and went back to the pier where a ship was waiting. Our long trip from the Hawaiian Islands to Eniwetok and from there to the Marianas was uneventful, in regard to any enemy encounters. Unexpectedly!

Four from Rigby High School

♦

Leaving Maui, I was leaning against the ship's rail, watching flying fish, when someone slapped me on the back. It was Orville Jones, a friend from Rigby, Idaho, our hometown! I was surprised, but not nearly so much as when Orville told me that another of our classmates, Frank Benson, was aboard. We began a search and soon located Frank, leaning against another of the ship's rails.

Wow! Three of us—from Rigby.

No. Four! Frank said that Lawrence Hansen was on the ship too.

We found Lawrence and he explained his presence. He had been with the Marines who attacked Tarawa in the Gilbert Islands, one of the deadliest battles of World War II. That brief campaign resulted in 978 Marines dead and 2,188 wounded. Lawrence had been wounded. While he was being treated for his gunshot wound, his combat boots were lost. For most Marines that would not have posed a significant problem. Not so for Lawrence. His boots were custom made to fit his large feet. The Marine Corps did not stock 16EEE size combat boots. Lawrence had been on Oahu since the Tarawa campaign, waiting for replacement boots! He was now heading back to the action.

The four of us spent a lot of time together from Maui to Eniwetok, then on to the Marianas, but I never saw any of them again after leaving the ship.

A few years later, not long after I had been honorably discharged from the Corps and had returned home, I was told that Orville's remains had been returned from Tinian. I left Ogden, driving alone, and went to Rigby to attend his funeral. It was a gut-wrenching experience.

I well remember Orville's mother, tears streaming from her red eyes, asking if her son had to suffer long. She was under the impression I had been present when he was shot—when he died. I hadn't been, but I told her he had felt no pain, didn't even know he'd been hit.

Orville's dad watched and heard that exchange, and he looked at me as though he knew I was lying to ease the mother's grief. That intense knowing look has remained with me ever since. It pops into my memory—in every detail—frequently. And it has for 65 years. I actually felt guilty that I survived, and their son didn't.

Of the four of us, two were killed, and the two of us remaining were both wounded twice. Not a good statistic, but evidence that four Marines saw a lot of action.

Eniwetok—Ships and Sharks Galore!

Arriving at Eniwetok, we were amazed to see literally hundreds of ships: troop transports, cargo ships, destroyers, cruisers, battleships, and even a couple of aircraft carriers!

It was hot aboard our steel ship. Morale was low, so we were given permission to swim. Gun mounts about 30 feet above the waterline were favorite diving platforms for those who had the courage (or stupidity) to use them. And I was one!

About three days later, the men had hit a new low in morale. We still dived into the water and clambered up cargo nets to dive again, but that was getting old. So the Marine commanding officer and ship's captain decided to boost morale by serving a widely announced (and eagerly anticipated) steak dinner. Frozen meat was removed from the huge freezers. As it thawed, the cooks trimmed it and prepared it for cooking. The waste was thrown overboard. That was a bad thing to do!

Shark fins pinpointed our ship from every direction. Swimmers from our ship and the surrounding ships hastily climbed their cargo nets. The sharks were in a feeding frenzy that caused the ocean surface next to our ship to "boil." It was quite a sight to see, and a good lesson for those aboard all the ships.

We didn't do any more diving or swimming during the remaining time at Eniwetok, and we never went ashore.

Bombardment of Saipan

◆

When we arrived off Saipan, a U.S. Naval bombardment was underway, together with attacks by carrier bombers and fighters. Occasionally there was a scorching wave of fire from napalm bombs.

Movies can't compare.

The noise, the smell, the "feel" of tons of armament were beyond my ability to describe. And you wouldn't want to be there!

It looked as though no enemy could survive that horrific assault. In fact, most of them had taken shelter deep inside the many caves on the island, and were quite safe! Thousands survived to greet the Marines who would soon be going ashore.

I was not one of those required to go ashore at that time. My turn would come later.

"And I Died for You Today, my Friend..."

◆

It is most fitting and proper that we honor those who died in the great battle of Saipan and in the other battles of World War II. Private First Class Carl Dearborn (address unknown) of the 4th Marine Division, which went over the Saipan beachhead, paid honor, eloquently, in the following poem:

"And I died for you today, my friend...On an Island called Saipan..."

Don L. Jardine, Ph.D.   Combat Marine at Seventeen

I Died for You Today
by
Pfc. Carl Dearborn

I died for you today on a far off Pacific Island.
If you are concerned, to say the least, I'll tell you who I am...
I'm the soldier and the sailor—I'm the airman and Marine...
I'm the life blood of your nation—you sent me to this scene...
I'm the one who loads the Amtracks... I'm the pilot, just as well...
I'm the dedicated corpsman saving leathernecks who fell...
I'm the trooper of the airborne, I'm the Seabee with a trade...
I'm the wiry American medic dodging steel to give first aid...
I'm the tail gunner in the airplane, I'm the crew chief and the crew...
I'm the cannonade and mortar man in the field defending you...
I'm the man of different races clinging to a rumbling tank...
I'm Catholic, Jew and Protestant, and I serve in every rank...
Call me Dominic, Smith or Kelly or pronounce my foreign name...
And regardless of my color—When I'm hurt, I bleed the same...
I'm Indian and I'm Mexican. I'm Polish, Dutch, Italian and Greek...
I'm every inch American and your freedom's what I seek...
I'm the southern boy from Florida, I'm the northern lad from Maine...
I've toiled in Georgia's orchards, and I've cut Montana's grain...
I came from every walk of life—from mountains to the slums...
I've lived, by God, through dust and drought, and I've prayed aloud for rain.
I've known hardship and depression; still I've watched our country grow...
But when Uncle Sam came calling I was proud that I could go...
I've watched demonstrations and the people who protest...
And I said "Thank God for freedom!"—my country's still the best...
So take your banners and your slogans. Raise your placards to the sky...
I'll defend your right to do it... Though in doing it, I'll die...
I'm your fathers—sons—and brothers...I'm the arm of Uncle Sam...
And I died for you today, my friend...On an Island called Saipan...

Apprehension

♦

Prior to going into combat, many Marines attended their respective religious services or sought a personal interview with the military chaplain for comfort.

Some Marines wore a cross on their dog tag chain, carried a talisman or charm of some kind to ensure their safety, or resorted to unaccustomed praying.

Many clung to the belief that "What is destined to happen will happen. Hopefully, not to me."

And there were always fatalists that "knew" they wouldn't survive *this* campaign. How could anyone know?

The preceding poem has special meaning for me. Not only because it was composed by a fellow Marine concerning the island of Saipan (where I served—and fought—for more than a year) but because the author put into expressive words the feelings most Marines had at one time or another. I felt that same way about Formosa (now Taiwan), a formidable island we had once been destined to assault. I "knew" I wouldn't leave Formosa alive. Fortunately, that campaign was not necessary.

I well remember occasions when fellow Marines, apprehensive about imminent combat, earnestly requested their closest buddies to convey messages to their survivors after the war, or when they left a watch, ring, locket, or some other memento with non-combatants to be given to their loved ones "If I don't make it."

There are civilian vocations which sometimes require partisans to face life-or-death situations: law-enforcement officers and firemen top the list. They can probably better relate to the combat Marine that rushes ashore amid deadly weapons fire and explosions. But I submit, their experiences are always comparatively of brief duration.

After the Marine emerges from the surf and crosses the deadly beach, he faces death every hour of every day—for weeks or months. And after his many experiences—the moments live on realistically and vividly in his memory *every day* for the rest of his life.

Incidentally, many Japanese soldiers wore "a belt of a thousand stitches" around their waist to ensure safety in combat. Each stitch on his belt was added by a relative, friend or patriotic countryman.

I own such a belt. It hadn't helped the enemy soldier from whom I removed it.

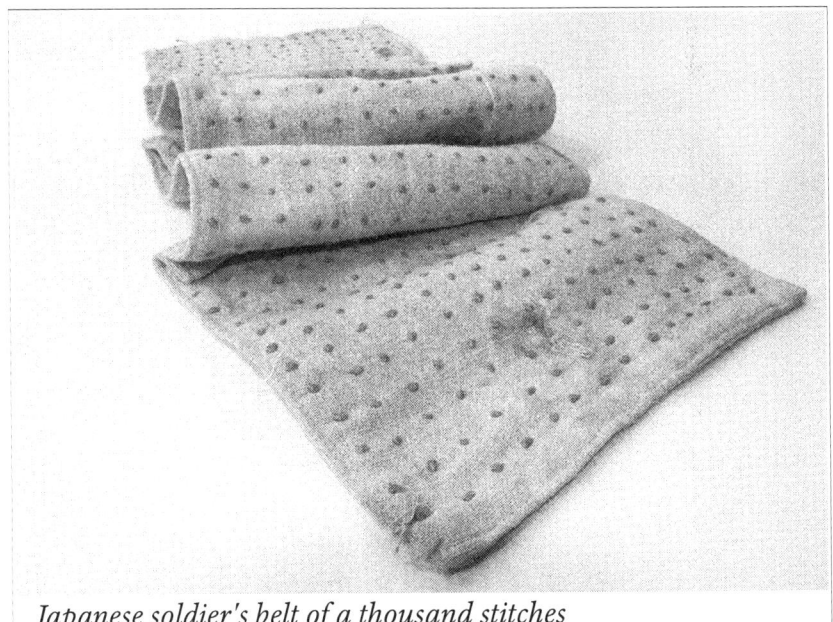

Japanese soldier's belt of a thousand stitches

Going Ashore—Tinian

♦

All the Marines aboard ship were headed for the cargo nets which we would climb down to the Higgins boats—landing boats that would take us to one of the Tinian beaches.

Imagine the enemy's heavy artillery shells exploding, creating high geysers in the ocean around your ship. You have donned full combat gear, loaded down with a full, heavily loaded pack containing canned and packaged food and some clothing—especially underwear and socks—toilet articles, a large bandage or two supplementing the first aid kit on your ammunition belt, a small shovel (called an entrenching tool), a bed roll with rainproof poncho or perhaps a shelter half, a steel helmet and helmet liner, weapon, ammunition belts heavy with bullets.

You carry as much ammunition as you can for the main weapon slung over your shoulder (carbine, B.A.R., M1 rifle, or assigned parts for a mortar or machine gun to be assembled ashore). There are grenades hanging from the front straps of your pack. You have a K-bar knife and/or a bayonet, a compass, two canteens full of water, and anything else you will need and can carry.

Even without the encumbrances, it is not an easy thing to lower yourself from the ship's deck, down rope cargo nets to the Higgins boat well below you. The small craft bucks up on one wave then descends with a shower of saltwater spray as it drops three or four feet, and then rises again on the next wave.

You have trouble breathing. At first you believe that it is due to the fear that is causing your heart to pound so rapidly. Then you realize how foul the air is from smoke and cordite—especially the cordite because it burns your breathing passages—all of which is leaving a strange, undesirable taste in your mouth.

The fellow ahead is going down the net, just as the landing craft is carried up by a swell of salt water. That is a signal for the man below him to drop into the landing craft. Too late! He drops as the boat descends with the receding wave.

Someone on the net cries out as a boot above crushes the hand he is using to keep from falling.

Landing personnel constantly urge everybody to move faster. Hurry! Those enemy shells are getting closer.

Your ship is firing heavy guns, as are many other nearby ships, lobbing shells that obviously are finding their targets. Columns of flame and smoke are erupting like small volcanoes all over the Tinian land area visible to you. You almost duck as low-flying carrier planes barely skim above the ships, engines roaring, eight machine guns blazing. Soon they will be dropping their bombs on Japanese emplacements, or perhaps fiery napalm creating waves of flame that splash over large swaths of land, together with clouds of black smoke that will add to the mass confusion of a Marine assault landing!

Thankfully, you get aboard the landing craft in one piece just in time. The coxswain pushes the throttle forward and the boat surges ahead as it is immediately replaced by the next landing craft, anxious for its fill of Marines.

If things go as planned, everyone aboard your boat will follow orders and keep his head below the gunwales until the ramp is lowered and you all rush forward.

Things never go as planned. You sneak a peek or two at the chaos around you. Wow! There are some landing craft that have been hit by enemy artillery. Some are smoking. Some are sinking. Several have sunk.

Shells are exploding everywhere, each one raising a fountain of ocean water as it explodes. Then you notice a body. Several bodies. Most are floating, face down, lifeless. Some are moving. They are Marine survivors attempting to swim to the shallow water at the beach. A few are discoloring the water around them with their blood.

This is real. You are living a nightmare.

Marines approach Tinian beach in Higgins landing boat.

No. You will not—cannot—understand what it is like by purchasing a movie ticket and settling down into a plush seat with your popcorn and drink to watch a Hollywood version.

We were there. And we were Marines. This is what we were trained for. We knew the eventual outcome before we left the ship to go ashore.

When the ramp on our Higgins boat dropped, we rushed through waist-deep water, anxious to reach land and lie prone next to any protective cover. That was the safest objective under the circumstances.

Bodies, all American, all Marines, floated past as we yelled and rushed forward. They added incentive for us to move as quickly as possible, which wasn't very rapid, loaded down as we were, in impeding waves of salt water that made it difficult to lift our feet. Bullets and shrapnel zoomed through the air, some finding their mark in friends, fellow Marines.

"We were there. And we were Marines. This is what we trained for."

Emerging from the surf onto the warm sandy beach, we hugged the ground while crawling toward anything solid that might provide temporary protection, or vegetation that might provide concealment.

The noise from guns and bombs in close proximity was deafening. Odors and smoke assailed our eyes, nose, and ears, mingling with the ocean's salty spray.

When we established the beachhead, major action moved slowly inland. The fighting became more personal as we crept and crawled toward the determined and desperate enemy in their camouflaged, fortified emplacements.

Sunset brought a heavy blanket of darkness. It had been an interminably long day and I had not even realized, as I did now, that I was thirsty. I quickly gulped the contents of one canteen, reserving the other, just in case a refill was not possible.

My second day on Tinian was much "easier," though there was constant action. An officer pointed at me and ordered that I accompany two other Marines as guards for a wounded Japanese prisoner. We were to take him back to a command post on the beach for questioning.

Traversing the same real estate we had crawled through the day before was not the safest thing to do. Inevitably, there were many bypassed enemy soldiers between the three of us and the beach. One of my companions had a simple solution. He had several ampules of morphine which he put to use. Without consultation or comment, he put our prisoner to sleep. Painlessly, quickly, and permanently.

We crawled under some bushes and waited an hour or so before turning back to rejoin our unit. I do not know what explanation was given for the failure to deliver our prisoner for questioning, but the three of us survived and we probably would not have, had we followed orders that were a death sentence.

My third and fourth days on Tinian proceeded on. One fire fight after another. I was tired, dirty, hungry, thirsty, frightened, and covered with flies and mosquitoes.

Tanks landing on Tinian beach

Wounded—First Purple Heart

◆

The next thing I knew, I was lying on a cot and had a terrible pain in my right leg. I did not know where I was. I sat up to check my leg and look around. That movement enveloped me in darkness, with an uncontrollable swirling reminiscent of the effects of ether prior to having my tonsils removed years before.

When I reawakened, a male nurse was sitting beside me repeating my name. Aware that I had regained consciousness, he introduced himself and answered my first question:

"Where am I?"

"You're in the Army hospital on Saipan."

"How did I get here?"

"I'm not sure. Most patients are being brought in from Tinian by boat or by gooney bird" (C-47 transport plane).

"Why am I in the hospital?"

"You caught some shrapnel in your knee."

So that's why my leg hurt!

Later, a doctor told me I had been wounded by shell fragments from a Japanese knee mortar. That name was given to a small enemy mortar because it has a curved base plate that Marines thought was intended to be rested on one's leg above the knee, while firing. Not true, but it certainly did a job on my knee!

I was wounded the first time on July 28, 1944, exactly three weeks after my eighteenth birthday.

Certificate awarding Purple Heart for wounds received at Tinian, Marianas Islands, July 28, 1944

Going ashore at Tinian

Enemy casualties in burned-out sugarcane field

Marines advancing in the Tinian jungle

Transporting a wounded Marine to the "hospital"

Saipan Hospital

◆

I spent four weeks in the Army field "hospital" on Saipan, following my wounds on Tinian. I was in a ward consisting of two large wall tents placed end-to-end, filled with wood and canvas folding cots (each with a wounded Marine), and four inches of mud for a floor.

Each ward contained approximately 32 patients and was assigned to two soldiers alternately working 12 hours on, 12 hours off. Our ward was watched over by an army truck driver and an army cook! They had been ordered to this duty, and a rough one it was.

This field hospital was located near Aslito Field, our air base on the southern end of Saipan and only three miles from the northern end of Tinian (which we could easily see).

Days were long in that hospital. You might imagine the noises: the injured Marines in pain and having nightmares; bandages being changed and medications administered during the nights; airplanes landing and taking off (ours); airplanes dropping bombs (theirs); anti-aircraft guns blasting away at the Jap bombers; changing of the guards; mosquitoes; sometimes moaning and screaming from our ward and other wards.

During this time, many of my fellow patients were transported stateside. Some died. Some, in addition to their wounds, had malaria, dengue fever or dysentery.

Ambulatory patients (very few) walked to the mess "hall" (tent) for meals. The rest of us had room service—slow service. Carts couldn't be used in the deep mud, so meals were carried, two or three at a time, to the patients.

My first concern upon being hospitalized was for my family. I didn't want them to receive a telegram before knowing I was really okay. I was much better off than most of my fellow patients.

So, when a Red Cross worker came through, I requested a pen or pencil, a sheet of paper, and an envelope. Sure! Two or three days later, when the Red Cross worker returned for a very brief walk through, he handed me two postcards. Each had American Red Cross printed across the message side in very large red letters. I'm sure it was intended that the writer would just write over that large red type, but I didn't. I was so disgusted I tore the cards in little pieces and never requested anything more from the Red Cross.

Incidentally, that same Red Cross worker spent most of every day in a nearby tent for Officers only—playing cards with the brass (the officers).

One day each week, every Marine that could get there went to a recreation tent to play bingo. Upon winning, a small bar of Hershey's Tropical Chocolate (slightly flavored chalk that couldn't melt) was awarded. The Marine was then dismissed. One small bar per week was the maximum allowed by that Red Cross worker. And he was being paid! Not just the regular salary, but with a large bonus for "hazardous duty in a war zone."

To Tinian and Back

◆

After 28 days in that Saipan field hospital I had reached my limit. The attending doctor approved my release. So, without any weapon or equipment, I followed orders to find my way (hitch-hiking) to Aslito Field where I was to board any available transport plane bound for Tinian. On Tinian I was to report back for duty with the 4th Division. And that is what I did.

I hitched a ride to Tinian on a C-47 Gooney Bird. I felt undressed without a helmet, pack, ammunition belt, and especially without a rifle. Upon leaving the C-47, I located some Marines and asked directions to a Marine Headquarters so I could report back for duty with the 4th Division. They laughed and told me that would be a good trick because my regiment (23rd Marines) of the 4th Marine Division had just left for our base camp in Maui! I had missed them by a day.

A Marine officer told me to get aboard another C-47 and return to Saipan. There I was to report to any Marine unit I could find—and my orders would catch up to me.

The plane I boarded was full of wounded Marines on litters, en route to the same field hospital I had called home for a month.

As the plane gained speed for take-off, it was swerving and bouncing like crazy, hitting and trying to avoid shell holes in the runway from the previous night's enemy bombing. A final bounce brought yells from many aboard, convinced as we were that the plane would hit a wing tip and crash. Not so. The plane lifted, miraculously, into the air.

Amnesia—Six Lost Days

◆

We landed at Aslito Field less than ten minutes after that interesting take-off from Tinian. I remember leaving the plane and walking to the main gate, where I intended to hitch a ride with a Marine vehicle, any Marine vehicle.

That is the last thing I remember for six days.

Doctors later said my dengue fever had probably returned, and that combined with stress, fatigue, and other factors had caused my consciousness to "shut down."

The next thing I remember, six days after leaving the airfield, I was seated at the edge of a pier in Tanapag Harbor, watching Marine watercraft approaching from Tinian. I had a Browning automatic rifle (B.A.R.), an ammunition belt full of ammo, a steel helmet, a canteen, a K-bar knife, and a pack!

As the Marines came ashore, I was directed to their commanding officer. He told me it was the 18th Regiment of the Second Division (Engineers) and I could tag along until my records caught up to me.

We boarded trucks that took us from that location on the west side of Saipan over to the 18th's new camp on the southeast side of the island, going through the tunnel (a natural arch) near the top of Mt. Topachau, the highest point on Saipan, at 1554 feet.

Most of the Marines were to spend the next few weeks in shelter halves (pup tents erected from two halves, each carried by a Marine). I had neither a "buddy" nor a shelter half. In fact, I had no shelter. So, a few Marines helped me locate three-by-six foot strips of corrugated tin (sheets of which were strewn all over the island, having been blown off huts and other small buildings by various shell explosions).

Most of these strips were perforated by many holes, from machine guns, rifles, grenades, shrapnel. Nevertheless, they provided some protection from the heavy rains when erected, like an Indian teepee around a tree. There was, however, no protection from the hordes of hungry mosquitoes that swarmed from about 45 minutes before sunset until 45 minutes after sunrise *(all night!)*.

Don Jardine provided a real feast for thousands of those little devils. I truly hoped they each caught and suffered from my dengue fever (an illness carried by mosquitoes).

Doctors attempted to determine my experiences while I was alone for six days. They even administered sodium pentathol, called a "truth serum," because anyone under its influence responds to questions with "truthful" answers from the subconscious.

The results were incomplete. I reportedly talked a bit incoherently about firefights with Jap soldiers, rain, the frustratingly painful bites of thousands of mosquitoes, swarms of flies, the horrendous stench of dead bodies (Americans as well as Japanese), fear, hunger, thirst, and fatigue.

When asked about the location of those experiences, I reportedly said "the jungles." They inquired concerning my acquisition of a helmet, B.A.R., ammo, knife, canteen, and pack. I told them I'd picked them up from Marine casualties located in the jungles.

Alone, I had a few "experiences" with Jap patrols as well as several individual Japs. All "in the jungles."

Incidentally, when I suddenly found myself sitting on that pier, overlooking the Pacific Ocean, I felt more alone, devastated, and abandoned than I had ever felt before. I was thousands of miles from home and, with the exception of the hospital personnel and a few patients, didn't know a soul west of the Hawaiian Islands. Nobody knew where I was, nor did it seem that anyone cared. I had nothing to eat or drink. It was hot. Every breath included a few flies. My head, body, legs, and arms were swollen from mosquito bites, and I still had a fever and fatigue from dengue!

My leg wound had nearly healed, but I still had almost constant pain in my right knee—and would the rest of my life.

Being alone is a feeling I'm unable to compare to any other, nor would I wish it upon my worst enemy (if I had an enemy). But I do wish I could describe it so someone, anyone, could understand the intensity of that terrible, unique feeling.

Saved by the Enemy

◆

One morning I crawled from my corrugated tin teepee experiencing a new and different pain in the upper groin of my right leg. Upon examination, I found a red streak running from the inside of my right knee up to my crotch. I showed it to the resident corpsman who immediately put me in a Jeep and drove to the hospital's surgical unit.

Doctors there confirmed the Corpsman's diagnosis—gangrene! I was taken directly to the surgery tent and placed on a table for amputation of my right leg.

I'd gone through the pain of shrapnel removal from my right knee, and now that the knee appeared to be healing, they wanted to remove the leg? I objected. Strenuously.

A chaplain was summoned by the surgeons. He explained that I could die from the gangrene and my permission for amputation was necessary in order to save my life.

As he was talking, air raid sirens began screaming and Jap bombs began falling and exploding. Our proximity to Aslito Airfield made us prime targets.

Unable to perform an amputation under those conditions and because wounded Marine victims of the Jap air raid were in more urgent need of medical assistance, the surgeons told me they'd have to "cauterize the shrapnel wound" until they could get back to me. I didn't know what "cauterize" meant. I learned!

Untrusting, I refused any anesthetics and watched as the doctors hurriedly cut away the dead flesh from my knee, used a red hot iron to cauterize the area, and filled it with sulfa powder. Then they bandaged it and I was returned by the corpsman to our camp.

That air raid wounded many Air Force personnel and Marines. There were so many that the doctors didn't order my return to surgery until four or five days later. By then, the temporary treatment they'd administered had been far more effective than expected. The red streak was gone and the knee was healing.

The surgeons decided the corpsman could watch the injury and, "if I was lucky," I might keep my leg after all, "but it will always be a big problem for you. You'll live with daily pain."

My prayers had been answered—and I still have the original right knee (with the pain), though my left knee was replaced over forty years later.

Souvenir Patrol

◆

The Marine Engineers I joined on the dock at Tanapag Harbor were good to me. They helped me in many ways. However, some of them expected my acquired combat skills in exchange. They wanted me to lead their unauthorized excursions into the surrounding jungles and caves (restricted areas) in search of "souvenirs".

Cave under flat rocks

On one such foray we found a cave-like space between two huge, pancake-shaped rocks. Perhaps 20 to 30 feet across, the space between them varied from about two to four feet, and extended back into the jungle. The bottom one was much shorter and the earth beyond it had been removed, creating a well-hidden, safe haven for several Jap soldiers.

The bodies of three Japs lay at the entrance in grotesque positions. It was apparent that they had been there for many days.

As I entered the narrow and claustrophobia-inducing entrance, I had to maneuver around several more corpses to check contents deeper inside the dark recesses.

I saw muzzle flashes as shots were fired at me from the darkness. I quickly returned fire with my BAR. The shooting ceased.

After checking to be sure none of the enemies' shots had found their mark, I crawled around and past bodies that had been charred from a flame-thrower.

It was obvious that no Americans had been inside this space because I located rifles, pistols, swords, bayonets, etc. Those popular "souvenirs" would have been taken by Marines had time and circumstances permitted.

I handed out the aforementioned items to the delighted engineers. Then, satisfied that there wasn't anything else worth taking, I crawled back out of the "cave," feet first. There wasn't room for me to turn around. I had decided not to go to the far rear of the cave, so I have no idea how many of the enemy had fired upon me. I just knew they would not be coming out.

As I exited the cave, several more shots were fired from the surrounding jungle. The engineers and I hit the deck. Fast! We all returned fire. Finally, when there was no return fire, I ran to the place from which we'd been fired upon and located the Jap sniper. Dead. He was carrying several items taken from dead Marines! Probably victims of his ambushes.

One of the engineers was creased by a Jap bullet and was bleeding profusely. Though in considerable pain, he was far more concerned about how he was going to explain the wound. All Marines had been warned about entering restricted areas and especially caves. The likelihood of engagement by hiding Jap troops was extremely high.

Two more souvenir hunts with the engineers were comparatively uneventful, but the third (and last) was a doozy!

Eight of us, all heavily armed, climbed through the jungle to the face of a cliff perforated by caves. I, of course, was in the lead.

After searching several caves, large and small, I entered one that was apparently much deeper than the others. The recesses of the cave were black dark. I was well aware that it was also potentially very dangerous because I was silhouetted by the cave opening behind me. I had that right! A shot was fired from the back of the cave, coming so close I could feel it.

Before I had reached a fully prone position, a war had started. Several weapons were being fired from the darkness and my engineer friends were returning fire. Some of those shots were far too close, but all I could do was press my body as flat against the floor and wall of the cave as possible and pray.

The firing stopped. We threw two fragmentation grenades that exploded at the end of the cave. Then we waited, listening, attempting to determine whether or not any of the Japs had survived.

No sound.

We waited.

Still no sound.

Finally, I inched forward and my companions did the same.

When we reached our adversaries, all four of them were prone. Three were dead, two of them from self-inflicted gunshots. The remaining Jap, dressed in a uniform much different from the others, was badly wounded and quite obviously dying. He was a Japanese naval officer!

When I searched him he struggled desperately to retain possession of a leather case held in his hand and with a strap over his head and on his shoulder. As he took his last breaths, I removed the case from him and took it to the entrance of the cave to examine its contents. They were not souvenirs. There were maps of Saipan and Tinian with a lot of Japanese writing on them and places marked with a variety of colors. Apparently color-coded locations of--infantry? tanks? fuel? ammunition? food? artillery? headquarters? aid stations?

Then I realized I had the same dilemma experienced by the wounded engineer!

The potential importance of the maps and papers in that naval officer's case was obvious. I knew I must turn it over to an officer who would have the contents evaluated for their military significance. That officer would no doubt want to know where and how the case was found.

Fortunately, we chose to return to our camp by hiking along the base of the cliff. We came to the road (there was only one in use on that side of the island at the time) and caught a ride with a truckload of fellow Marines. I worried. I believed I would inevitably face the questions of where I had found the leather case and what I was doing in a restricted area. I didn't want to get into that serious trouble, nor did I want to place my engineer friends in jeopardy of "military justice."

There were two Marine officers riding as passengers in the cab of that truck. I placed the Jap case and its contents in their hands as my companions and I dropped off the truck near our camp.

I've often wondered what the papers in that case contained. There is no doubt they were of military value but I was relieved that no explanation had been necessary.

Adventures such as this were no doubt the cause of orders being posted restricting such activity. The following is one such order that I kept:

```
CMcG/dee                 SECOND MARINE DIVISION, FMF,
RESTRICTED                    IN THE FIELD.
                                                    17 April, 1945.
DIVISION MEMORANDUM)
NUMBER........87-45)     RESTRICTED AREAS.
```

1. THE FOLLOWING EXTRACTS FROM ISCOM LETTER, FILE 370.2/40 (C), DATED 6 APRIL, 1945 ARE QUOTED FOR COMPLIANCE BY ALL MEMBERS OF THIS COMMAND:

"2. Pertinent information regarding the enemy situation on Saipan follows:

  a. During the six week period ending 241800 March 1945, the following enemy personnel were killed and captured:

  (1) Japanese military killed _____ 156
  (2)   "   "   captured _____ 92
  (3)   "   "   civilians taken into
                           protective custody _____ 107

  b. In February 1945, the headquarters of an organized band of Japanese numbering between 350 and 370 persons was discovered within 400 yards of an Engineer base yard.

  c. OPs are currently sighting bands of as many as thirty to fifty Japanese. A large number of the Japanese are armed.

  d. The most recent casualty as a result of enemy action was a SeaBee shot and killed on 18 March 1945 while souvenir hunting in a RESTRICTED area.

  e. Japanese still at large on Saipan are not confined to RESTRICTED areas. They or their bivouacs are often found close to our installations from which they pilfer food, water and clothing. Specific warning is issued against visiting any isolated section away from settled areas except when in line of duty.

  f. Entering or approaching caves in any part of the island is extremely dangerous and is prohibited except in line of duty.

3. RESTRICTED and OFF LIMITS areas are patrolled. It is the policy of this Headquarters to direct disciplinary action in cases of unauthorized presence in such areas. Copies of the attached map designating these areas will remain posted on bulletin boards and will be made readily available to all personnel.

4. It is directed that unit commanders make known to every member of their commands the above information and the areas designated RESTRICTED and OFF LIMITS. Reports of compliance will be consolidated by major echelons and staff sections listed on page 51, Memorandum Number 1, cs, this Headquarters and submitted to this Headquarters prior to 201630 April 1945.

5. The sole object of this communication is to prevent the useless loss of life to American soldiers, sailors, and marines.

                    BY COMMAND OF MAJOR GENERAL JARMAN:

                                        C. E. RICHARDSON
                                        Lt. Col., A.G.D.
                                        Adjutant General

Order prohibiting souvenir hunting in restricted areas of island

Ordered to Rifle Company

♦

The engineers were a good outfit, but I was ready to move on when my orders finally arrived. I was assigned to 3-I-6, 2nd Marine Division. That is—3rd Battalion, "I" Co., 6th Regiment. This was an outfit with an outstanding history which included having been granted a permanent award of the *Fourragère* by France during World War I.

Looking north from Saipan Camp.

We set up base camp on a Saipan ridge. Looking to the north, we could see the tents of the 8th Marine regiment. I did this drawing from the west end of our camp, as a visual record censors would approve. Note the ocean in the upper right-hand corner.

My new outfit was located high up (west) on a ridge that ran from east to west, perpendicular to the north/south spine of the island.

We were surrounded by jungles, but could see the 8th Marine Regiment on the next ridge north of us.

Bombers (B-17s, then B-29s) taking off from Aslito Field to bomb Japan flew low over our area. Daily and nightly. Hundreds of them. What a roar! What a sight!

For a period of several months, Jap planes bombed every night, and fighters strafed about every third day.

Washing Machine Charlie, a Jap bomber, came late at night on harassment raids. We were "entertained" by searchlights and tracers from our anti-aircraft guns. Charlie eventually was shot down, terminating that particular "show."

We often saw parachutes blossom as Jap airmen vacated their damaged planes, but none landed in our area, even when aircraft were hit almost directly above us. Most of the 'chutes drifted to the west side of the mountains. Seabees there (Construction Battalions) frequently had visitors from the sky.

Reportedly, most Japs fired their side arms as they neared a landing. Seabees returned fire and the Japs were usually killed before they could be captured.

Enemy Caves

♦

During my many combat patrols on Saipan and Tinian, I was never more apprehensive and fearful than when entering a cave. Both islands were replete with them.

You can well imagine the silhouette of your body, the target you'd present to an enemy as you moved into a dark cavern, their eyes accustomed to the dark, yours unable to see into the darkness.

I always went into a cave as rapidly as possible, fully expecting to be fired upon. And with good reason—I often was!

Some caves were quite small, but every one of them was a possible haven for a hiding Jap soldier, or many. Most caves were large and it was not unusual for one to be occupied by several of the enemy seeking refuge from Marine patrols.

We usually called out "Dai tay koi" (come out) before going into a cave. If there was no response and we felt certain someone was in the cave, we'd throw a fragmentation grenade inside.

When possible, especially for very large caves, we'd "hose it down" with a flame thrower.

Many times I've seen Jap soldiers, on fire, run out of caves. As a rule, they had one hand over their eyes and another over their crotch. They didn't run far.

It was always a pathetic and horrific sight, accompanied by almost inhuman screams and horrendous, unforgettable odors.

Enemy soldier in foxhole, killed by flamethrower

Wet Combat Patrol

♦

Our thirty-two-man platoon of Marines was nearing the end of a miserable six-day combat patrol. It had been raining for three consecutive hours as the sun set below Saipan's mountains to our west. Darkness was descending rapidly and we had yet to locate an acceptable place to spend the night.

Two recent firefights with Japanese Army holdouts had certainly alerted all enemy combatants in the area to our presence. We wanted and needed to reach nearby caves where we could sleep in an easily defended and dry situation.

Weighed down by packs, weapons, and rain-soaked clothes, we struggled through the dripping wet jungle, finally reaching foothills with nearly vertical cliffs perforated by numerous caves —some no doubt occupied by Jap soldiers!

Selecting one of the largest caves, Pfc. Henry and I slowly and cautiously made our way to its entrance. After listening carefully for a minute or so, Henry ran inside pressing himself against the wall to minimize his silhouette should anyone be watching from the cave's dark recesses. I followed seconds later, doing the same.

A quick search convinced us the cave was unoccupied, so I signaled for the Marines outside to enter.

It felt wonderful to get into that dry cave after being in a drenching downpour for so long. We were all soaked to the skin —and cold! That was a unique experience on this tropical island.

Posting a guard at the cave's entrance, we lay on the floor and promptly fell asleep. We were exhausted.

Sometime during the second guard's two-hour watch, we were all awakened by sounds of a struggle. A Jap soldier, after entering the cave unaware of our presence, was fighting desperately with our guard. Another Jap, apparently trying to help his companion, was close behind. And he was armed with a rifle complete with bayonet.

Corporal Sundell killed the second Jap with one shot from his .45 caliber pistol. Others of us rushed to assist our guard. However, when the Jap he was fighting apparently realized there were several Marines in that cave, the Jap turned and ran outside, into the darkness. We didn't pursue him.

The Jap soldier shot by Corporal Sundell had a beautiful pearl-handled knife with an eight inch blade still in its scabbard. Sundell became its new proud owner.

We left the cave as soon as it became light enough to see. This was the final day of our patrol. We'd sleep in our own tents that night. Thankfully.

The clothes we wore were still far from dry when we left the cave. Rain had ended but the wet vegetation we forced our way through continued soaking us until the heat of the tropic sun dried both the jungle and us. I welcomed the warmth. It had been an especially miserable and interminable night.

Our platoon leader suggested we search the caves around us for Jap soldiers. Knowing Sundell's shot and noises from the struggle had been heard by every enemy in the area, we made other suggestions.

Locating a trail that afforded much easier transit through the jungle and cane fields, we made our way eastward toward the coral road where we would rendezvous with a Marine Corps truck. It would return us to our permanent camp several miles south. There we would change into clean, dry clothes, eat a hot meal and sleep, sleep, sleep.

Thinking of War

♦

Fortunately, we had no more encounters with the enemy on the patrol just described. However, we did come upon two distantly separated places where recent firefights were in strong evidence: maggot-filled bodies of Jap soldiers with the indescribably strong stench that is *never* forgotten, rusting weapons, food cans—some empty, some full, some American, some Japanese.

I couldn't help but wonder what had occurred at each place. How many had died there? Were there many wounded? Wounded seriously? And if I had been there, would I have been a casualty?

I thought about parents of the combatants, American and Japanese. What about their siblings, relatives, sweethearts, wives, children? Each "small" firefight affected countless people, not just those directly involved but others literally thousands of miles away!

Marine encounters Japanese family.

What about my own actions? I had killed several young Japanese, some probably no older than I. Did I feel guilty or remorseful? Perhaps—very briefly. Then I thought about more than two thousand of my fellow Americans killed at Pearl Harbor during Japan's dastardly sneak attack, civilians as well as military. And what about the documented cruelties by Japanese military personnel in their P.O.W. camps, on the Bataan Death March, during the infamous Rape of Nanking, and the starving, torturing and murder of thousands! Terrible atrocities.

And I remembered friends lost during combat and others wounded so badly it would affect the remainder of their lives (and the lives of those who loved them).

I am quite certain there was very little introspection among my fellow Marines, but I was always taught to have compassion and exercise forgiveness. My companions were more accustomed to abiding by the adage "an eye for an eye." Even so, we all knew what we had to do and did it.

It was only recently (2012), while reading author Laura Hillenbrand's best-selling, fascinating book *Unbroken*, that I learned several things that, even now, ease my conscience regarding my killing of many Jap soldiers. On Tinian the Japanese held five thousand Koreans, conscripted as laborers (p. 354). Apparently afraid that the Koreans would join the enemy if the Americans invaded, the Japanese *murdered* all five thousand Koreans! (p. 358). There were rumors that the Japanese had retaliated against Chinese civilians for sheltering the Doolittle men, but at the time people didn't know the true extent of it—the Japanese *massacred* an estimated quarter of a million civilians!

And many Japanese military and P.O.W. guards were convicted of horrendous cruelties against American military prisoners, including beheading, in the War Crimes Tribunals that were held after Japan's unconditional surrender.

Later in the war, during my occupation service in Nagasaki, Japan, I met and came to know several Japanese individuals and families. Without exception, they were all very polite, considerate and hospitable. Even so, scriptures tell us that "almost all men, as soon as they get a little authority, as they suppose...will immediately begin to exercise unrighteous dominion."

American Prisoners of War were starved, tortured, worked to exhaustion, and even killed. They weren't permitted to write to their loved ones, who frequently didn't know if they were dead or alive. Red Cross and other packages intended for our P.O.W.s were confiscated and used by their captors.

Unbroken is a true "World War II story of survival, resilience, and redemption." Survivors of a bomber's crash spent forty-six days on a small rubber raft bumped by numerous large sharks, and spent the balance of World War II in Japanese P.O.W. camps staffed by brutal guards.

Saipan's Charan Kanoa sugar factory remnants. Note the narrow gauge train tracks.

Don L. Jardine, Ph.D. Combat Marine at Seventeen

Disabled American tanks and enemy corpses

Mail call: Infrequent, but always welcome

Flame-throwing tanks help Marines destroy enemy opposition

The fight moves over Jap soldiers where they fell

Marine shelter halves (small 2-man tents) and killed enemies in the aftermath of a Jap Banzai attack

Garapan, Saipan's capitol, destroyed by naval and aerial bombardments

The Ninety-day Wonder

♦

When I was transferred from the 18th Marines (Engineers) back into a rifle company, I was placed in a platoon as a Browning Automatic Rifleman.

I was pleased to join permanently a group of young men who were good Marines and soon became like brothers. We came from widely scattered states and extremely diverse backgrounds, but I had full confidence in each and every one. We were completely dedicated to helping each other. Sometimes our lives depended on it.

We all liked our platoon leader. He was a career Marine officer, a lieutenant, well-trained, intelligent, dependable, and fair. He knew how to lead. His numerous combat experiences enabled him to make quick, correct decisions. He cared for each of us. He even *looked* like a Marine Corps officer. His image on an enlistment poster could have been very productive. However, he was wounded by a Jap sniper while leading us on a Saipan combat patrol just a few weeks after I joined the platoon. The wound was serious and necessitated his return stateside for medical help.

He was sorely missed.

His "replacement" was something else. He was what everyone called a "ninety-day wonder."

As a result of nearly a full year of study in a community college, he'd been accepted into Officer's Candidate School, and in three months was commissioned a second lieutenant in the U.S. Marine Corps. We were at war; we needed officers!

His employment experience as a shoe salesman didn't prepare him very well for his new responsibility. He came to Saipan directly from the U.S. mainland, so I'd be very surprised if there was even one member of our platoon who wasn't far better prepared (by hard-learned combat experiences) to lead us. Add to that his appearance. Though tall and slender, he was gangly and somewhat awkward. In fact, the consensus was he looked more like a Girl Scout leader (my apology to Girl Scout leaders) than a Marine Corps officer.

Now if you note some negative prejudice on my part, please read on and consider this: I soon had a very major reason for prejudice. Our new platoon "leader" decided not to rotate point man assignments as our previous leader very fairly had done. Point man is, by far, the most dangerous assignment in any rifle platoon. A point man moves well ahead of his unit and is therefore the one an enemy sees, and shoots, first. So when he announced that Don Jardine would henceforth serve as permanent point man, the lieutenant made it sound like an honor. He said his decision was based upon my high school R.O.T.C. training, my combat experience, time overseas, and superior eyesight. Sounds good, doesn't it? And Harry James Henry would be my permanent assistant. He would be following between me and the platoon.

The lieutenant's explanation would have probably been accepted without controversy except for reports from several of his fellow officers, friends of ours. They told of conversations in the Officers' Club detailing different reasons for his choices.

Henry was selected as my assistant because he was prone to spout off his feelings concerning almost any subject whether it was "politically correct" or not (usually not).

Jardine was chosen point man, permanently, because the lieutenant hated Mormons! And I was not only a Mormon non-smoker, non-drinker, and non-profaner, but I was also from Utah, that den of iniquity where—according to him—residents were not Christians!

When I denied membership in—or even knowledge of—a "Mormon" church, it angered the lieutenant. I explained that I was a member of The Church of Jesus Christ of Latter-day Saints. What was the name of the church he claimed affiliation with? He knew the church to which I belonged bore the Savior's name. Mormon is a nickname given by non-members who belong to Christian churches quite similar to ours. We are all Christians, and in our church we are taught to respect the rights of Catholics, Lutherans, Baptists, Presbyterians, Jews, atheists, Muslims, agnostics, Buddhists, and others, to worship or not worship as they choose.

In our lieutenant's mind (and church) that teaching was not reciprocal.

Henry and I were well out in front of the platoon on every combat patrol because, to our lieutenant, we were the most expendable.

Fortunately for me, God did not share the lieutenant's view. Through God's grace, both Henry and I survived, and I am here writing this book over sixty-five years later.

Forgotten Guard

♦

On one of the two occasions our battalion boarded a ship for transport to aid fellow Marines fighting on Iwo Jima, I was ordered on guard duty ashore. The officer of the day and sergeant of the guard took me in a jeep to a storage dump notorious for raids by Japanese army holdouts.

The dump, located a mile north of the ship and at the edge of a jungle, was an isolated repository for a wide variety of military supplies neatly boxed and arranged according to priority for quick and easy access.

I assumed my post at 1800 hours (6:00 p.m.) and was scheduled to be relieved at 2400 hours (12:00 midnight). It would be six long hours, alone.

As darkness fell, my imagination continually played tricks on me. Every movement, regardless of cause (land crabs, wind, shifting fabric of a box cover) deserved immediate attention. Was that movement actually a Jap soldier? What about that shadow? Was it there a minute ago? Did it move? What is that sound? Could it be the enemy?

As one might suspect, time dragged by at a snails' pace. I looked at my watch every half hour or so. No! Each time only five or ten minutes had passed!

Holding my M1 rifle ready to use, I strained to see into the black night, and listened intently for any unidentifiable sound.

Midnight came...and passed. 0100 hours (1:00 a.m.) came...and passed.

Nobody came to inspect the guard, as required by regulations.

The hours passed slowly, giving the voracious mosquitoes ample time to feast.

Morning light came slowly because I was on the West side of Saipan, shielded from the sun by the intervening mountains. Thankfully, the sun brought considerable relief from mosquitoes. As it rose above the mountains, clouds of flies took over!

According to my watch, it was nearly 1000 hours (10:00 a.m.) when I saw a jeep approaching. Great! I was about to be relieved. Wrong! The driver was a naval officer.

I gave him a snappy salute as he exited his vehicle. He came up to me, returned the salute and asked what Marine outfit I was serving with. Then he asked if it was customary for me to serve on guard duty without shaving.

I replied, "I shaved just before I came on duty, sir."

Looking surprised, the naval officer asked, "And when was that?"

"It was 1800 hours yesterday, sir."

"Are you telling me you have been on guard duty for sixteen hours? All night? Alone?"

I replied, "Yes, sir!"

"Did anyone come to check on you?"

"No, sir."

"Son," he said, "Get in my jeep."

I replied, "Sir, I can't leave my post until properly relieved."

He said, "I'm a lieutenant commander in the United States Navy. You *are* properly relieved."

He took me to the ship, ordered a sailor to accompany me to sick bay and said, "I'll see you in a few minutes."

The sailor escorted me to the ship's sick bay, pointed to a bunk with white sheets covering a 4" thick mattress, and said, "That's where you'll sleep." Then he had me undress, pointed to the showers and said, "Have a warm shower, then put on these pajamas and this robe."

Wow! The showers were not salt water (as I'd come to expect on shipboard) and the clean, soft pajamas felt wonderful. The plush white robe was luxurious. I had just lain down on that heavenly soft mattress when a group of naval and Marine officers entered followed by the two men who had driven me to my guard post.

If you haven't heard of "King for a Day," I can tell you what it's like. I was treated royally!

After apologies from several of my visitors, I was treated to a hot roast beef meal, a glass of real milk and a large dish of delicious ice cream! Then I was allowed to sleep for 12 hours or so. Had I reported the incident to our commanding officer, a few career Marines would have suffered severe punishment. And they knew it!

We were never taken to Iwo Jima. Our unit was being held for the Okinawa campaign.

Okinawa Invasion

April 1, 1945 was D-Day, the invasion of Okinawa (also referred to as L-Day, to distinguish it from the Normandy invasion).

It was also Easter Sunday, April Fool's Day, and my mother's birthday!

The 3rd Battalion, 6th Regiment of the 2nd Marine Division had been held in reserve for the Iwo Jima campaign. Now, we were on a ship approaching Okinawa.

Moving onto the main deck from the troops' quarters below, I looked up toward an ever-increasing roar. It was a Jap Kamikaze plane, diving directly at me! I stood, mesmerized, fully aware that there was no place to hide, nothing I could do. I was about to meet my Maker.

At the very last moment, and for no apparent reason, the pilot of that Japanese suicide plane drew back on the controls, lifting the plane over my ship and crashing it into an LST (a specialized cargo ship) a couple hundred yards away.

It is probable that the Jap pilot quickly changed targets, believing the LST was preferable to our troop ship because there were tanks, half-tracks and trucks on its top deck.

There is absolutely no doubt, that Jap pilot's quick decision seconds before he died was my life saver.

The kamikaze plane crashed into the LST with an explosion. That ship sank completely in less than ten minutes.

Our battalion boarded landing craft and, after assembling, moved toward Okinawa's beaches. As our landing crafts neared the sandy beaches, they suddenly all turned around and went back to the ships! I don't remember any shots being fired by Americans or by Japanese.

The landing crafts were lifted back aboard the ships and we returned to Saipan. That was the extent of our participation in the Okinawa Campaign. We had been used as a diversion to pull away some of the Japanese defenders from distant beaches where the main invasion was taking place.

It was a great relief to all of us that we were not called on to engage enemy troops on Okinawa. However, we knew it was to be a brief respite. The planned invasion of Japan was next and we expected it to be a more intense campaign. By far!

We had been briefed on what would be expected of us. A huge, 4-by-10-foot topographical display had been shown to us, so we knew where we would land and what we could expect.

Trucks met us at Tanapag Harbor and transported us back to our base camp on the east side of Saipan.

Precious Water

♦

While we were away during the attack on Okinawa, Japanese army holdouts moved into our tents and made good use of our water point. We knew, because we surprised and killed several of them upon our return. All were heavily armed.

Our base camp on Saipan was well located. At the bottom of the hill upon which our tents were erected was our treasured "water point." It was a natural spring of constantly flowing, cool, clear, clean water. We carried that water in five gallon containers up the steep hill several times each day that we were in camp.

Safe drinking water was vital in the tropics. We perspired a great deal, inevitably, and replacing that hydration required drinking water frequently and in large amounts.

It was difficult to assure that the water we consumed from untested sources was not contaminated, despite our use of halazone and other purification tablets. Filling canteens from streams was dangerous for several reasons. Channeling enough fresh rain water into the small opening of a canteen was difficult and took time we seldom had.

Of course, the Japanese also prized good water. Some of the Japs were exceedingly reluctant to give up that prized water below our camp. Though we had reclaimed our tents, Jap soldiers frequently returned to the water point during the nights to fill their own containers.

After several serious confrontations and the enemy's tripping of booby traps we had set, we decided to ambush their encroachments by posting guards on the water point throughout each night.

When our turn came to serve as guards, Henry and I pushed our way into the heavy foliage around the water source, spread our ponchos on the damp ground and settled down. We wouldn't be relieved until four long, dark, quiet hours passed.

Quiet? We hoped! Long? Inevitably!

Because we could hardly see each other in the darkness, we were confident of our concealment.

The sky was black but sparkled with millions of blinking stars. And it was quiet. Very quiet. Except...what is that? Did I hear a twig snap? Are those bushes rustling? Was that a bird call...or a Jap soldier? Did I hear a voice? What is that crawling toward us? Are those movements caused by a breeze I can't feel...or by a Jap?

Imagine the tension, the fear, the constant expectation of a face-to-face encounter with someone who will kill you—if you don't kill him first. Dramatic? Yes. True? Absolutely.

Land crabs were always scurrying across the ground nearby and were a realistic explanation for the noises. We hoped!

There! I did hear a sound. I heard someone and so did Henry.

We raised our weapons, B.A.R.'s, and without saying a word pointed them toward the sounds. We had visitors! How many?

My heart was pounding so hard I knew it could be heard. Or was that Henry's heart I heard?

Two figures approached, silhouetted against the stars. One began filling a container with water while his companion, obviously waiting his turn to fill his containers, kept whispering in Japanese. The only words I understood were "danger" (a-boo-NA-ee), "water" (me-zoo), "Marine" (reek-SEN-ta-ee), and "hurry" (ee-SO-gay).

I was applying increasing pressure on the trigger of my weapon, about to kill the intruders, when Henry beat me to it. He killed both Japs with a burst of automatic fire from his B.A.R.

Marines on top of the hill, awakened by Henry's firing, called out to us as several scrambled downhill to give assistance, if needed.

Their help was not needed.

Guards were posted at the water point every night for the next two weeks. Well-armed Japs seeking water were killed on the second and third nights, but none thereafter. The word got around, apparently, to all enemy holdouts in our immediate area.

That was fine with us.

A Saipan Patrol, and Pondering the Planes

◆

Every third week my platoon clambered aboard a truck that took us from our base camp to the north end of Saipan. We knew that region well, having patrolled it many times. And it was still heavily occupied by Japanese Army holdouts. They sought concealment in the heavy jungles and in caves that varied in size from that of a small closet to ballroom size. Many were nearly hidden by dense vegetation.

Japanese army holdouts, bypassed during the campaign, were a constant threat. They raided our bases at night, trying to acquire everything from food and clothing to weapons, ammunition and medical supplies. It was not uncommon for them to fire upon staff cars and other non-escorted vehicles, or even upon individuals or small groups of Americans. Our patrols were doing everything possible to suppress their activities, permanently.

White dust arose around and behind our bouncing vehicle as it sped along Saipan's one road—a white, crushed-coral road. The heat was severe.

When the truck reached our destination and we disembarked, the driver lost no time heading back to base camp, well aware that we were all in a dangerous area susceptible to enemy fire at any time.

We quietly filed into the nearby jungle, heavily loaded with the gear and ammunition we needed to spend the next six days searching for the enemy.

Moving as cautiously and unobtrusively as possible, the platoon followed as Henry and I led them toward the face of a limestone mountain spotted with caves. We would search for the enemy in as many caves as we could check before dark and, hopefully, find a large, unoccupied cave where we could spend the night in comparative safety.

Each of the three squads was ordered to search specific caves. And though evidence of recent use was found in five or six of them, none of the caves was presently occupied. Thank goodness.

We located a suitable cave in which we could spend the night, posted a guard at the cave's entrance and bedded down.

The platoon leader awakened those of us who were still asleep at dawn's first light. We ate our C-rations, donned our gear and moved out.

I checked my compass frequently to keep us on the planned heading. All three squads continued searching caves, apprehensively but fruitlessly.

To remain in our assigned search area, we moved downhill toward the nearby jungles and coastline.

I came upon the lighted stub of a cigarette and called the platoon to a halt. We formed a skirmish line, then resumed our advance knowing that no enemy had been bypassed, so was therefore still ahead of us. Probably close by.

Neither Henry nor I had seen anything in the heavy vegetation we were fighting our way through, so it was a surprise when Private Zimmerman, behind us, fired his M1 rifle, then shouted, "I killed the S.O.B!"

The Jap soldier probably was not alone.

We moved ahead as rapidly as possible and began hearing the sounds of people crashing through the jungle in haste.

Coming upon a small stream, one of our squads came under enemy fire. The rest of us rushed toward the shooting to assist our fellow Marines. When I came upon the source of the shooting, two Jap soldiers were lying, dead, in the shallow stream. They had just been shot by the squad members we were attempting to help.

A sudden roar startled us. Low-flying B-29 bombers, heading for their targets in Japan, zoomed directly overhead, one after another, three hundred or more of those huge superfortresses.

The canopy of vegetation hid the bombers from sight, but it was eerie to try comparing the airmen's war with our own. They couldn't hear, see, smell, or sense the Japanese individuals to whom they were delivering death. They would finish their bombing assignment, return to their airfield, shower, enjoy a hot meal, and retire to beds with white sheets, minus mosquitoes, before we would complete our day's combat patrol and return to our cave and C-rations.

Our close combat experiences were similar to those of Army soldiers in their various locations. However, we knew no sailor and no airman was fighting as we were.

Though our objectives were the same (locate and exterminate the enemy and end the war) there were three distinct forces, each fighting its own war—on land, on and under the seas, and in the air.

The incongruity of the various situations was really incomprehensible. And it was the source of numerous disagreements between members of different branches of the military, even among close friends and relatives.

There was a somber silence after the bombers passed us. We couldn't hear a sound.

Henry and I motioned for the platoon to move out and we proceeded forward as quietly as we could. A half-hour or so passed and we were still in dense jungle, moving slowly and quietly, when a very loud, heart-stopping scream stopped every one of us. We stood silently, listening, for several minutes. Then we continued forging our way through the jungle.

As we came upon a well-traveled trail, we saw a Jap soldier. He was dead, but still bleeding. His throat had been cut!

Travel was much easier on the trail and we hurried along, expecting to locate the Jap's killer or killers at any moment. We were apprehensive, but failed to sight any adversaries before reaching our cave.

We never learned why that Jap soldier was killed, but it was apparent he died at the hands of one of his fellow countrymen.

Booby Trap Explosion
◆

Some Marines called it jungle, others called it hell! But whatever the dank, verdant area was called, it had to be penetrated to reach a designated spot on our map. There we would rendezvous with a truck for transportation back to our base camp. And we were late!

Movement was extremely difficult. Vines, roots, thorns, bamboo, trees, shrubs, palmettos and other impediments grabbed at our flesh, clothing, packs and weapons. There was absolutely no way we could force passage without creating enough noise to alert even the most inept Jap soldier. And we were tired. Exhausted. We had reached a point where the prevailing attitude was, "Oh, what the hell!" We just didn't care if the Japs heard us. And they did hear us!

Sleep was a luxury we looked forward to. If we weren't shooting at the enemy, they were shooting at us. We were deprived of sleep, or even rest, by the almost constant noise of gunfire and explosions, combined with nighttime flares that lit up the jungles for blocks around, creating black shadows that danced as though they were shape-changing creatures.

This patrol had begun 64 hours ago, and we had dispatched at least 18 enemy holdouts in brief firefights at the cost of only two minor casualties: flesh wounds that only required field bandages.

In the dark, we constantly referred to our compasses in order to proceed in the correct general direction. We were anxious to take the shortest and fastest possible route to the truck that we hoped was still waiting for us.

Whoom! An explosion briefly lit the immediate area, accompanied by a scream of severe pain. A Marine had stumbled over a trip-wire, setting off a booby-trap. That was a signal for every Marine to "hit the deck!"--and it's a good thing we did.

Japanese rifle fire, grenades and knee mortar shells tore through the surrounding vegetation. Several suicidal Jap soldiers came crashing through the underbrush, shooting, brandishing swords and bayonets, shouting in Japanese and yelling "Banzaii". They were inebriated from *sake* (Japanese wine).

I fired at the closest Jap. Bullets from my Browning Automatic Rifle ripped him apart, as they did the two who followed him.

My fellow Marines were as busy as I was, and just as effective. We quickly sent a dozen enemy soldiers to their imperial heaven.

None of the Marines was injured except the one who tripped the booby-trap. He had several wounds from shrapnel and had to be helped by two buddies as we continued our trek to the truck rendezvous.

A Booby Trap Detected

◆

I was pushing through one of Saipan's dense jungles, feeling very vulnerable as I led my Marine platoon on another combat patrol. And I *was* vulnerable, but I had 31 well-armed Marines on my heels following me.

Suddenly there was a definite movement ahead. It was on one side of the weakly distinguishable path I was following, not more than ten or twelve feet in front of me.

I stopped.

The movement stopped.

I raised my Browning Automatic Rifle slightly and fired a short burst.

All hell broke loose!

Return fire clipped leaves nearby as enemy bullets zipped past me and past my assistant, Harry James Henry, Jr.

My shots had brought Henry running up to me. The rest of our patrol was close behind.

There were unmistakable sounds of men tearing rapidly through the jungle but we were still unable to see the fleeing Jap soldiers. Even so, some of our bullets were finding their mark. Outcries of pain, some in Japanese, were sufficient evidence of that.

In this area there was no cause for concern about firing upon innocents. There weren't any. We were in wild country and there were no civilians or structures of any kind for miles around. And there were certainly no other Marine patrols

Any sighting, any sound was sufficient reason for us to fire at its source. And we seldom fired without bringing return fire upon us.

Moving again as rapidly as possible, I passed a badly wounded Jap soldier—apparently in his final moments—and nearly stepped on a dead one.

Henry and the other Marines kept firing into the surrounding jungle.

Private Zimmerman, some twenty feet behind Henry and me, shouted, "I've been hit!"

A Jap rifle bullet had put a clean hole through the upper part of his left shoulder and he had to be helped along as we pushed forward, toward the waning enemy fire.

Entering an area of far less density, we could see our adversaries desperately running through open places, toward the protection of cover and concealment.

They didn't make it.

Every one of the Jap soldiers we could see was brought down by the platoon's withering fire. Eleven of them.

The platoon gathered for a well-deserved break, careful to stop inside concealing stands of trees, vines, bushes and grasses.

Zimmerman was attended to and we were enjoying the respite from immediate danger when a familiar sound struck fear into every one of us. An enemy mortar had fired a shell that flew toward us and exploded quite close by. A second shell followed, then a third. But they exploded, thankfully, farther and farther away. It was apparent the Japs could not pinpoint our location, so we remained where we were.

Some of the men searched deceased Japs laying on the ground near us, pocketing a few rare souvenirs—a belt of a thousand stitches, knives, a couple of Samurai swords, some small Japanese flags, a few photos, military emblems, etc.

After half an hour without any mortar shells exploding around us, we continued the patrol. We knew there would be other encounters before we were done.

Unlike the experiences of Vietnam Marines years later, we seldom located booby traps. When we did, they were usually under dead bodies, American as well as Japanese, set to explode when the corpse was moved. Nevertheless, the point man (me) had to constantly be aware of anything suspicious that might be the cause of immediate death or injury.

Coming upon a rather large vine across our path, slightly different in color from neighboring smaller vines, I signaled for the patrol to take a break.

Henry wanted to know the reason. We examined the vine without touching it, followed it under some thorny bushes and found the end threaded by the Japs through the activating pins of three American fragmentation grenades! Had anyone tripped over that vine they would have died very suddenly, and anyone nearby would too, or at least been struck by grenade fragments.

I can't explain it so anyone can fully understand, but experienced combat Marines develop a "communication system" that often warns of imminent danger. It's almost like a tiny voice that lets one know "Stop! There's danger ahead!" I learned to listen and obey that warning voice. Frankly, I believe that is why I am still alive.

Other Marines have shared that same awareness.

Zimmerman's shoulder was becoming increasingly painful, so we decided to attempt an earlier-than-scheduled contact with the truck that would return us to our base camp. There we could have a doctor give Zimmerman the professional attention he needed.

We came upon a small stream and waded downstream. It was easier travel.

Seeing a Jap soldier ahead, I raised my weapon and was about to fire. A shot wasn't necessary. He was dead.

In and near the stream were several more dead Jap soldiers. Henry came up beside me. A Jap moved. Henry shot him. The enemy soldier had been seriously wounded earlier, probably a day earlier. He had remained with his dead companions, too badly injured to travel. It made us move more slowly and cautiously, now aware that other Japs could have survived a firefight with a Marine patrol (or vigilantes) that preceded us much earlier.

Rain began to fall. It poured. I had to refer to my compass frequently to maintain direction. We could come upon armed enemies at any moment without warning. I even began imagining movements as the downfall hampered our progress and vision.

It was still raining when we came upon a very welcome sight. It was the white coral road that led back to our base camp! But there was no truck.

We found concealment under vegetation at the roadside and sat, drenched and swatting mosquitoes, for almost an hour before we heard the truck approaching. We were all delighted, especially Zimmerman, as we clambered into the back of the truck and sat in the rain while the truck turned and headed toward dry tents, dry clothes, warm food, and welcome cots.

Several buddies in our patrol congratulated Henry and me for locating the road. They admitted they would have found it difficult to do, especially during a tropical rainfall, through jungles that were often dark and nearly impenetrable.

Zimmerman was taken to the Division hospital. The bullet that had hit him passed completely through his shoulder. His doctors said it was a miracle he was not permanently injured.

I believe it was a miracle that Zimmerman was the only one injured, and that nobody was killed.

It was also a miracle that Henry and I were able to locate and disarm the Jap booby trap.

Cold Combat Patrol

◆

It was early morning and Saipan was getting a heavy shower. I don't know what the temperature was, but I was wet, cold and itching all over from mosquito bites.

Our 32-man platoon was pushing through a field of sugar cane on the second day of a five-day combat patrol.

The Marine platoon we relieved told us of several firefights —skirmishes with bands of 20 to 30 Jap soldiers. They estimated extermination of no fewer than ten of the enemy, with many others wounded. Three Marines had been wounded, one severely. The patrol looked tired, certainly ready to return to our base camp and hot food, showers, and rest.

Their warnings kept us alert despite fatigue, hunger, unidentified noises, slipping in the mud, and cuts from sharp leaves.

Hearing a sudden rustling of sugar cane nearby, I fired at the sound. The patrol came to a halt. Every Marine was listening intently with a finger on his weapon's trigger.

I moved toward the source of the sound I had fired at and found a dead Jap. Before I could check him out, there was rustling in the sugar cane ahead of me, to the right, and even behind me!

With my B.A.R. on fully-automatic, I fired toward the sounds as my fellow Marines did the same.

There was no return fire, at first. But there was chaos with obvious movement in the surrounding sugar cane, epithets in Japanese and in English, a painful scream and the noise of several rifles plus more than a couple of hand grenades—Japanese and American.

The cane was eight feet high and difficult to move through.

Suddenly and unexpectedly, we came to the end of the sugar cane. Jap soldiers, some wounded, were exposed as they rushed toward the thick concealment of the nearby jungle. Some were firing their rifles at us.

Marines poured return fire upon the routed enemy, sending several to their imperial heaven.

Nobody on the patrol was injured but we still had three more days to search that wild area of northern Saipan.

We were unaccustomed to being cold. Most days on tropical Saipan were sunny, with an average temperature in the 80s. It was easy to imagine an island paradise if peace prevailed, but it was not peaceful then. Far from it!

Barefoot Marine

It was not uncommon for our platoon to spend nights in the jungle when on combat patrol. As darkness fell, we would tie a mosquito net over our heads and lay down on the ground with our unprotected hands between our legs to help keep them from exposure to those flying pests.

Several days often passed before we'd remove our boots. Sometimes the soles of our socks would remain in the boots and our feet were white and translucent from being wet so long! It was called jungle rot, and was very painful. A purple medication was supposed to cure the condition, but seemed totally ineffective.

I was trying to get my boots on one morning when we came under fire from Jap holdouts. A Marine had spotted a Jap sniper moving into firing position. When he shot the sniper, other Jap soldiers began firing at us.

Barefooted, I sought concealment and returned fire with my B.A.R.

We had no idea how many of the enemy we had encountered, but thirty-two of us mounted a good volume of firepower in their direction.

I had no time to put my boots on before I was ordered to make a flanking move, approaching the Japs from a direction that would give me the element of surprise.

Pfc. Oman was ordered to do the same from the opposite direction. (He was wearing his boots.)

Frankly, it was more than uncomfortable to move through the jungle with nothing on my feet but a few cuts and burrs. Very painful!

As I approached the source of enemy firing, I lay flat on the ground and wormed my way forward as quietly and unobtrusively as possible. I pushed apart a small bush to see what was ahead of me. There was a Jap soldier less than six feet in front of me firing his rifle!

Reasoning that one more shot among the many being fired would go unnoticed, I took aim, careful to make it a fatal shot. It was.

I laid there for a few minutes before wiggling through the thick vegetation that concealed more Japanese. Passing closely by two dead Jap soldiers, I came upon a small defile concealing and somewhat protecting three more Japs. Removing a fragmentation grenade from my ammo belt, I pulled the pin, released the activating spoon, waited a second or two, and then tossed it directly on target, killing all three.

There was no way for me to know how or what Oman and the other Marines were doing.

Finally the shooting stopped. The surviving Jap soldiers retreated deeper into the jungle as Marines assessed the skirmish. Pvt. Maitland had sustained a flesh wound in his upper right leg but the bullet missed the bone. Pfc. Oman had shot two Jap soldiers and three more were lying dead among the carnage.

The entire incident lasted fewer than fifteen minutes. I located my boots but minor injuries to my feet precluded wearing them for two days.

Some weeks after my release from the Marine Corps, Utah friends suggested we go swimming in the Great Salt Lake. They had learned something I didn't know. That lake's salt water, though initially painful, actually cured problems I was still having with my feet. Quickly! All symptoms of jungle rot disappeared within three days, and never returned.

English Speaking Japanese Prisoner

♦

As night fell I was bone-tired. Unfolding a mosquito mask, I placed it over my head and tied it around my neck. Then, laying down on the damp jungle ground, I curled into a fetal position with my bare hands between my legs in a futile attempt to protect them from voracious mosquitoes.

I fell asleep instantly.

A sudden staccato of rifles and automatic weapons burst all around me, but I was weary and slow to become fully awake. Actually, despite the very dangerous situation, I wondered where I was and what was causing that sleep-interrupting noise.

My platoon was in the third night of a combat patrol searching the northeast end of Saipan for marauding, well-armed enemy soldiers. And we were taking heavy fire from a band of Japs we'd been harrying for nearly three days with little rest and practically no sleep.

As I tried to shake the cobwebs from my sleep-starved, befuddled brain, I clutched my B.A.R.—my Browning Automatic Rifle—and crawled under nearby jungle vines and vegetation seeking concealment and cover from the explosions around me.

The first of my 20-round magazines emptied almost instantly as I returned fire on full automatic.

Shouts in Japanese and English added to the din with numerous epithets in both languages. There were cries of pain by Japanese and Marines. The latter called for the corpsman. (We only had one navy corpsman attached to our unit.)

I felt the breeze of several near-misses as bullets and shrapnel whizzed past from friends and foe. Their positions were difficult to ascertain in the dark and the confusion seemed to last much longer than the four to five minutes that were later estimated.

When the firing finally stopped and a shroud of silence settled over us, three Marines had been wounded—not life threatening. In the morning we located one dead Jap soldier, left behind by his fellow soldiers, and a heavy trail of blood. We had obviously wounded some enemies that would be incapable of more fighting in the near future, if they survived.

Forcing our way through thick jungle with our three wounded buddies, we headed toward a rendezvous point where we were to meet a second patrol from our battalion.

Exiting the immediate jungle area, we came upon the face of a high, vertical cliff, spotted with several caves of various sizes. As we approached the entrance to a huge cavern, we saw the telltale sign of Jap occupancy—a pile of fresh snail shells, the food Jap soldiers had resorted to, by necessity or preference.

With Marines on both sides of the cave entrance, we called "Dai tay koi!"—an order to come out. The response was quick and a total surprise. In good English, a Jap soldier replied, "Go to hell!"

We warned that grenades and flame throwers would be used if necessary. The reply was repeated.

We threw a thermite grenade and two fragmentation grenades toward the rear of the cave after holding them three or four seconds following activation (to preclude any opportunity for the Japs to return them).

Following the explosions we called out again. The English-speaking Jap responded, saying he was the only survivor and again refused to exit the cave.

Having heard that Guadalcanal Marines had often faced a similar situation, but were nevertheless successful in taking some prisoners, we resorted to the same ploy.

"If you don't come out we'll kill you!"

"Go ahead. I want to die for the Emperor!"

"After we kill you, we'll place your body inside the carcass of a pig!"

That brought immediate results.

In the religion of many Japanese, dying for their Emperor reaped rich rewards: high honors, beautiful virgins and treasures in the hereafter. But pigs were not allowed into their imperial heaven, so they believed a body buried inside the carcass of a pig was stranded on earth for eternity.

The Jap came out in a hurry.

Japanese soldier

Usually the limitations of language disallowed the use of such psychology, but that time it enabled us to capture the only survivor of six soldiers in that cave. And he spoke English, making him the source of easier and important military information.

In most combat situations, Marines knew enough Japanese to say "Come out," "Sit down," "Danger," "Stand up," "Hurry," "Stop," "Advance," "Don't shoot," and other important commands, thanks to a Japanese language guide and Japanese phrase book issued by the Marine Corps.

These language books must have been written by American-Japanese civilians because many phrases began or ended with "kudasai" (please) or "arigato" (thank you).

While in combat or holding Japanese prisoners in custody, we certainly didn't want to be polite! To the Japanese that was a sign of weakness. It was far more important and effective to command. "Thank you for answering," "Please don't shoot," "Please drop your weapons," "Thank you for coming out," "Please tell the truth," and similar phrases just didn't cut it!

Occupation forces in Japan could be—and were—more polite. Marines quickly learned greetings in Japanese, such as "Good morning," "Good afternoon," "Good evening," "Good night," "How are you?" "I am well, thank you," "My name is..." "Goodbye," "Do you understand?" "How much is it?"

Counting in Japanese is easy and learning enough Japanese to get by doesn't take a lot of time, yet it was very helpful.

Marines even reached a point where they recognized some Japanese calligraphy. That was especially helpful and useful later in Japan.

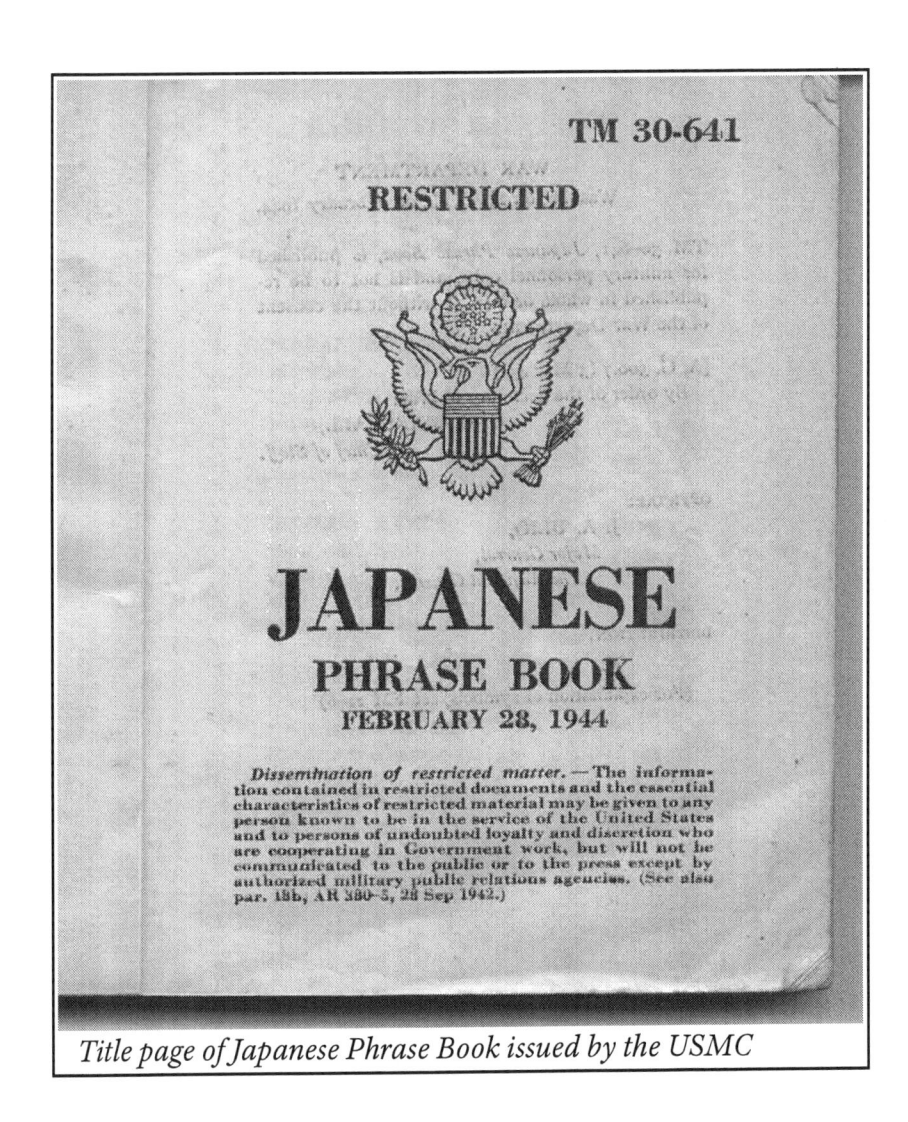

Title page of Japanese Phrase Book issued by the USMC

"Torpedo Juice"

Officers of the 2nd Marine Division on Saipan apparently gave no thought to Marines who didn't imbibe alcoholic beverages, and demonstrated little concern for those who did.

No more than once each occasional month, every Marine was issued two bottles of cold beer. No soda water—though a cold, non-alcoholic drink would have been eagerly awaited and appreciated in that hot climate.

Those rare beer events had meaning for me only because friends washed my clothes for two weeks in exchange for the beer issued to me. I have never used alcohol.

The alcoholic content of beer was insufficient to satisfy Marines who had long been accustomed to regularly using far stronger beverages. Therefore, when sailors from vessels docked temporarily in Tanapag Harbor made their way to the east, wild side of Saipan, with bottles of alcohol to sell, it wasn't uncommon for groups of Marines to pool their money or war souvenirs, and purchase all they could get for the cash and items they offered. That was a direct violation of Division orders.

One six-man group of enlisted Marines (officers had their own sources) purchased two bottles of alcohol from a submariner for "only $60"—per bottle!

Unfortunately, the alcohol was "torpedo juice," *not* intended for human consumption.

Three of the imbibing Marines endured excruciating pain for several days before they died, despite stomach pumping and other desperate measures to help them. The other three also experienced severe pain but survived. All three survivors were permanently blinded. However, that isn't the end of the story.

The Commanding Officer of the Division was irate. He ordered every man who wasn't on absolutely necessary duty to attend the funeral for the three dead Marines.

Using a loudspeaker, he reviewed widely promulgated orders and repeated the specific Division order regarding use of alcohol. Hesitating for several minutes, he then said, loudly and distinctly, "There will be no burial with honors today. No customary twenty-one gun salute. No taps. And, the families of these three men will *not* receive the $10,000 National Service Life Insurance they paid for! As far as I am concerned, the dead Marines committed suicide."

Hesitating again, for dramatic effect no doubt, he said, "And with regard to the three Marines who lost their vision as a result of disobeying my orders, they are being returned to the States today. Not to a veteran's hospital, but to medical facilities of their choice. They will be dishonorably discharged from the U.S. Marine Corps and will *not* receive any benefits."

There was very audible murmuring from the hundreds of Marines assembled there. Many felt the Commanding Officer was unfair, totally lacking in compassion. Others agreed with the actions taken.

If a Marine learns nothing else in boot camp (if you can imagine such a possibility) he does learn to obey orders. That, in my humble opinion, is what makes Marines so effective in combat. Being, on average, younger than militants in the Army and Air Force, we may have been too dumb to consider alternatives when given an order. Marines jump when told to jump. They don't wait to ask "Which direction?" "How Far? or "Why?"

And when the Regimental Commanding Officer issued an order for Marines to abstain from using non-issued alcohol, we all knew he meant *not a drop!*

Rations and Flies

◆

We had two types of rations.

First, we had C-rations, which were in two small cans. One contained crackers, lemonade, bouillon, sugar, coffee, candy, toilet paper and four cigarettes. (Imagine all of that in one small can). The second can held food intended to be warmed. In the tropical climate and with very little time to eat, we seldom warmed the Beef Stew, Chicken and Noodles, Spam with Potatoes, or Corned Beef Hash. In fact, we often discarded the last two. We were so tired, as a rule, that food was low on our list of priorities.

Second, we had K-rations, which were much easier to carry and generally preferred. They were in a waxed box about the size of a Cracker Jack box (or today, a video cassette). They were marked B for breakfast, L for lunch, and D for dinner. We seldom had a choice, merely grabbing the number of boxes we felt we'd need or could carry. About 7.5" X 4" X 2" thick, the waterproof boxes held, for breakfast: Nescafe, ground ham and eggs, a "candy" bar, a package of toilet paper (a priority item), sugar, hardtack, matches and four cigarettes; for lunch: lemonade powder (which could help conceal the taste of polluted water), sugar, four cigarettes, crackers and a tiny can of soft cheese; for dinner: a can of "food" to be heated (we seldom did), a "candy" bar, sugar, Nescafe, and crackers.

And, bananas and coconuts were quite plentiful.

My buddies did many good things for me, knowing I'd give my cigarettes to them. I have never used tobacco in any form.

Lack of water was often a problem, though it rained frequently. I tried to channel rainwater into my canteens (we each carried two)—rather than get it from the streams. When the latter was necessary, I always tried to scout upstream a hundred yards or so (though the danger of doing that alone was high).

One's thirst can diminish rapidly when dead bodies are found in the drinking water! And that happened, American as well as Japanese bodies. Cadavers in the tropics are inevitably covered and filled with flies and maggots. Some were still leaching blood. The stench is almost unbearable, and the thought is difficult to deal with.

Blowflies and maggots infest bodies of fallen Jap soldiers

Timmons Revenge Patrol

◆

Literally hundreds of huge B-29 Super Fortress bombers, some with obvious battle damage, were descending from their daily delivery of bombs to major cities in Japan. One by one they thundered low overhead in their customary landing pattern for Saipan's Aslito Field just to the south, or for their base on Tinian Island only three miles beyond.

Marines were so accustomed to them and their deafening noise that they went almost unnoticed as we washed our mess kits from evening chow and trudged wearily uphill toward our tents. It had been a rough day and we were looking forward to lying on our cots and getting a good night's rest.

Before we had time to settle down, orders came for our Marine battalion to "Saddle up, we're going into the field." Field, of course, meant Saipan's jungles.

We soon learned our 3rd Battalion, 6th Regiment of the 2nd Marine Division wasn't alone. All battalions in our regiment were under the same orders. This was something special. Even the heavy mortars and machine gun companies, together with flame throwers and half-tracks prepared for combat. Something big was up!

With our full gear, we scrambled aboard trucks that sped northward on a definite mission.

The dust hadn't settled nor had we come to a full stop when we were ordered out. Other trucks screeched to a halt and disgorged their troops. We all rushed to join those who had preceded us, anxious to learn the reason for this unscheduled, hurried, mass effort.

We were told that Corporal Timmons, a near legendary hero in the Second Marine Division, had been killed on combat patrol a few hours earlier. Veteran of campaigns on Guadalcanal, Tulagi, Tarawa, Saipan and Tinian, Timmons was well-known for his heroic actions in battle. He had been awarded the Silver Star for bravery and had at least two Purple Hearts.

As word of Timmons' death was reported to Second Division headquarters, they also received orders for Timmons' return to the United States to participate in a War Bond tour! He never learned that after many months fighting the Japanese, he would have flown home *the next day!*

The Second Marine Division commanding officer was intent upon immediate retribution. He ordered a full-scale action.

Well-armed Marines were dispersed around the jungle-covered hill where Timmons' patrol had been attacked.

It was too near dark to begin our search for the Japanese Army holdouts that day. We'd wait until dawn. During the night one of our large mortars fired a shell at somewhat regular intervals to keep the enemy awake. It did, of course, keep us awake too.

The Japs were audacious. After each mortar shell exploded, they fired a long burst from their machine guns in reply. That served to inform us they were prepared to fight, and had the means—weapons and ammunition—to do so.

At dawn we ate our K-rations and prepared for the assault. The mortars fired smoke shells at the hill where the Japs were hiding. Half-tracks had been firing their heavy artillery at the caves. With smoke to cover their approach, Marines ran to the base of the hill. Then they began a systematic search of all the caves. My platoon was ordered to a high ridge to sever possible routes the Jap soldiers might use to escape.

The orders were to search every inch of that densely covered hill, including every cave. Doing so, with literally hundreds of well-armed, battle tested Marines took less than an hour. During that short time we accomplished our mission and were confident that every Jap soldier on that hill (and there were many) had been dispatched to his imperial heaven. Timmons was avenged.

In the Sugar Cane—The Most Dramatic Scene of my Life

◆

The day was still young. I suspect other rifle platoons were given the same orders we were given: "Patrol the surrounding area to locate and eliminate all Japanese military."

A captain (commanding officer of my company) was in charge, as our regular platoon leader had taken half of the platoon to the Office of War Information Radio where the Japs had been attacking in search of food. The captain's name was McPeters. He was the imitation of Napoleon. Short and mild-looking, he tried to make up for his short stature by giving loud commands. We called him "Bunny."

Dead Japs were lying all over. A radioman and a new corpsman who had just arrived from the States were very nervous. We had hiked about a mile in comparatively open terrain and it was very hot. We were all tired.

Upon reaching a small plateau, Bunny called a halt and everyone went from a vertical to a horizontal position immediately. Bunny dropped his equipment and walked with the Sergeant to the edge of the plateau. In about ten minutes he called to us asking that we report to him immediately and to bring his gear.

As we walked toward them all hell broke loose. One of the Marines had sighted two Japs preparing some food at the edge of a stand of sugar cane. He fired his B.A.R., killing one and wounding the other.

The wounded Jap escaped into the cane. Bunny was yelling for his weapon. As point man I led our platoon essentially

Sugar cane field on Saipan

downhill, toward the distant ocean. We formed a skirmish line and slowly moved forward into a large field of sugar cane. We did not realize how tall some of the cane was because it was growing in a defile.

Several of us started working our way through, west to east. We reached the other side without finding anything, so we started again at the north end. I was in the center of the line.

About halfway through the cane I noticed blood on the ground and on the cane in front of me. I called the others to a halt and followed the trail of blood with my eyes. It ran behind me and as I turned I saw the Jap. He was lying in a curled up position in back of me. I had walked within three feet of him but the heavy growth of sugar cane and grasses had obscured him from view.

Under orders, I shot him.

Suddenly, a single Jap broke through the cane ahead, running for his life. He disappeared in the heavy foliage before a shot could be fired. Bunny ordered us to swing our line toward him and continue our patrol.

We hadn't moved more than a hundred yards in our search for him when, directly ahead of me, I saw two bare feet, toes pointed toward me! I immediately imagined those feet belonging to a Jap seated behind a machine gun aimed at my mid-section!

Bunny and Lieutenant Alley, leader of our platoon, were about 30 feet away, standing on a dried mud dike to observe our search. Though not directly in my line of fire toward the Jap (thankfully), I knew they'd chew me out if I fired without warning. But I also knew those feet were attached to a Japanese soldier who would delight in using me as a target.

I shouted, "Here's a Jap. I'm going to fire!" And I did. I fired three shots from my B.A.R. as I charged the Jap yelling at the top of my lungs like a warrior Indian. I was expecting the Jap to fire at me or to come charging.

The Jap came into full view as he fell, shouting in Japanese. Two of my bullets scooped away the flesh from the top of one leg; the other bullet did the same on his other leg. All three bullets struck just above the Jap's knees, gouging away a trough of flesh that looked like the watermelons women carve out as a receptacle for fruit to serve at a family's summer picnic.

I noticed that he had no weapon and about the same time became aware of another Jap yelling and moving through the cane. I swung my rifle around to fire but saw that it was a woman and she had her hands in the air. I called out, "Don't shoot! It's a woman!" In one hand she had a purse. I took it from her thinking it might contain a weapon.

The Jap soldier and a woman civilian had built a grass shack in that field of cane, and it was well concealed. He was undoubtedly a Jap soldier "holdout" and she was his companion —and, I might add, probably a very delightful one. She appeared to be about 20 years old and quite attractive. She was nude to the waist and only a few rags partially concealed her from the waist down. And she was screaming, shedding tears like a faucet, holding her hands over her eyes. She had probably seen the gruesome wounds to her companion's legs.

In a few seconds Corporal Sundell came to my assistance. We took the wounded Jap and the woman to the knoll where Bunny stood. She was crying hysterically and we feared the noise might bring other Japs. Bunny guided her to one side so she couldn't continue staring at her companion's wounds.

Then began the most dramatic scene of my life. This memory often replays itself in terribly realistic nightmares—in full color. It is mental baggage, like that carried by most men who have been in hand-to-hand combat situations.

The Jap looked down at the huge wounds in his legs and pointed to a Marine's rifle pleadingly, indicating a desire for the Marine to shoot him.

Bunny saw the gesture, agreed with the Jap's wish and, not wanting any more noise, ordered us to use a knife or bayonet to oblige.

Japanese soldier and mate. He bowed!

None of us wanted to comply. Bunny looked at me, "Use your bayonet on him Jardine." I replied, "I have a B.A.R. sir." Men with Browning Automatic Rifles did not have bayonets. I did not volunteer that I had a K-bar combat knife with a sharp, 8-inch blade.

Corporal Sundell said, "I'll shoot the ___." Sundell aimed his rifle. The Jap smiled.

Then, just as Sundell's finger began to squeeze the trigger, the Jap sat up! He placed his hands together, smiled, and bowed to each Marine standing nearby. Including me! Still smiling, he lay down, crossed his arms, and Sundell fired.

The woman stopped screaming.

Bunny was concerned about the woman. He was afraid some of his men might take advantage of her. So he kept saying, "She is pregnant. Leave her alone."

Enemy Encampment

◆

Proceeding on the patrol with our barefoot female captive wearing a Marine's shirt (at Bunny's insistence), we left the cane field and had perhaps gone through half a mile of dense jungle when we came upon a relatively open area. At an abrupt rise in the ground we were overlooking a small stream in the valley below. Several Jap soldiers were prone in rest, some were bathing, and two were scrubbing a Japanese boy about seven years of age.

All their rifles were stacked in one place!

As we spotted the Jap soldiers, they saw us. We, all 32 of us, started firing as some Japs attempted, unsuccessfully, to reach their weapons.

Two Japs tried climbing a vertical embankment, clawing desperately to reach the jungle concealment above them. They were easy targets.

As we ran toward the Japs, I saw a sight I'll never be able to erase from my memory. And believe me, I have tried.

The two Jap soldiers who had been bathing the little Japanese boy were lying, dead, in the stream. Between them was that little boy with the upper half of his head missing. It was lying near him, like half a cantaloupe.

More mental baggage!

Twenty-five Jap soldiers and the boy died within two minutes.

If the situation had been reversed, I am confident they would have done what we had to do. Even so, that scene (as many others) has replayed itself in my memory and my nightmares for the past sixty-eight years. That incident, together with Sundell obliging the wounded, bowing Jap soldier, has plagued me far more than I can put into words. Every detail comes back frequently and repeatedly during realistic nightmares I abhor.

Blinded by Enemy Hand Grenade— Second Purple Heart

♦

We continued our patrol from the scene of that massacre, and we were in a hurry. We had to reach a rendezvous point where trucks would take us back to our base camp.

Still "on point," I came across a large "room" in the jungle. The vegetation had been hacked away, creating an open area of about thirty feet in diameter, completely hidden from the air and difficult for anyone passing by to see.

On the far side of that jungle "room" was a large Banyan tree, the kind of tree with a trunk that begins about eight feet above the ground, supported by several huge roots with sufficient room between them to easily and effectively conceal several men.

On the ground in front of that tree were three bulky Japanese army packs!

I waited for Henry (Harry James Henry, Jr.) to come up. When he asked why I had stopped the patrol, I pointed to the Jap packs.

He immediately understood, as I had, that whatever those packs contained, Japanese holdouts would not leave them unattended.

The owners were watching us!

Henry said, "Let's go get 'em."

I said "Go to hell."

He offered to go first so I asked him what he was waiting for. Time went on and we were both in the same position, sitting on our heels, rifles across our knees, waiting and listening. I turned to ask Henry what he wanted to do. He was raising his rifle. I turned to see where it was pointing as he fired. A Jap fell prone to reveal two companions behind him. They were hiding between the large tree roots. Henry got them too.

Blinded by grenade

Then all hell broke loose. Bullets were whining past us, chopping vines down above us and to the sides. We heard the plunger of a Jap grenade pop and saw it trail from the base of a tree. It hit the foliage overhead, and fell between Henry and me. We knew there was not time to throw it back, so we dived prone to the ground. The grenade exploded. We were less than six feet apart.

Rifle fire was clipping leaves around us as we both sat up and looked to see if we'd been hit by grenade fragments (you can't always feel it due to adrenalin). We looked each other over. No blood, so we returned fire. All of this happened in seconds.

The platoon behind us rushed forward to give assistance. Corporal Cipullo was shouting, "I'm hit!" He had a half-dollar-size hole through the palm of his left hand from grenade shrapnel.

Five Jap soldiers no longer needed the contents of their packs.

Henry and I had flung ourselves to the ground when we heard or saw the Jap grenade coming. Very fortunately, we fell into a depression which probably saved our lives. We felt very lucky to have escaped without injury.

As we resumed our trek toward the truck we prayed would still be waiting for us, my vision began to blur. Henry said his was too and he kept complaining, "My back hurts like hell!" He asked me if he was bleeding. "Negative," I replied.

By the time we reached and boarded the truck, we both were alarmed, unable to see objects even close by. And we couldn't attribute it to the falling darkness. Henry insisted he had been hit in his back by shrapnel. Removing his shirt disclosed no wounds from shrapnel, but a 10- or 12-inch long burn! He had fired his weapon so rapidly that it burned him when he slung it over his shoulder, the red hot barrel on his back! Adrenalin had kept him temporarily unaware of the injury and the pain.

Upon reaching camp, fellow Marines helped Henry and me off the truck and led us to the Navy corpsman's tent. He called for a doctor, who treated Henry's large and painful burn, washed out our eyes, inserted a medication, and bandaged us. Then we were placed in a double tent—a small tent inside a larger one—to prevent any exposure to light.

The prognosis was discouraging.

Three long, terrifying days passed before the bandages were removed. We were still unable to see, so the procedure was repeated. Another three days dragged by before the bandages were again removed. This time, both Henry and I could see a small penlight the doctor passed to the side of our face. We were delighted when the bandages were not replaced and we were assured our vision was returning.

Doctors checked us daily in our dark tent for the next several days. Eventually, and very thankfully, our eyesight was restored.

Doctors explained the reason for our frightening experience. They said our vision wasn't affected immediately following the grenade explosion due to abundant adrenalin which provides protection from severe trauma. Then as the danger passed and the adrenalin wasn't so active, shock from the exploding grenade, concussion trauma to our optic nerves, became apparent.

We didn't suffer flesh wounds from the exploding grenade because we had so quickly dropped to the ground, fortunately in a low spot, and the shrapnel flew over and beyond us. That is why Corporal Cipullo was wounded. He was in the open, twenty feet or so behind us, when the explosion occurred.

If you want to experience a never-before appreciation for your vision, have your eyes bandaged. I recommend for 72 hours but I don't believe you will wait that long. If it's only for 24 hours, when you remove the bandage you will experience a vastly greater appreciation for your eyesight and will have far more empathy for those without it. You also will have a better understanding of how frightened Henry and I were.

Because neither Henry nor I shed blood from the blinding effects of that exploding Jap grenade, our platoon leader, believing that bleeding was necessary for anyone to qualify for a Purple Heart, didn't request it for us. He was mistaken. It was a combat injury and I was awarded the Purple Heart, my second, many years later.

I hope Henry was awarded one too. He deserved it.

Jap Air Raids

♦

On Saipan, for several months we had an enemy air raid almost every night—and about every third day. The day raids were generally Jap fighters, the night raids, bombers.

We watched the night raids like most young people would watch a ball game or fireworks. There were plenty of the latter, with searchlights stabbing into the darkness, illuminating the Jap bombers, and with tracers from our anti-aircraft guns streaming toward their targets.

Some of our guns fired explosive shells that burst at specific altitudes. The brilliance of their explosions was awesome, the noise was deafening, and they shook the ground.

We knew we were quite "safe" because the Japs were targeting the airfield, storage areas and ships in the harbors. However, that was not always the case during daylight hours. The Zeros strafed troops as readily as other targets.

"In the field" it was usually quite easy for us to find concealment because there was thick jungle in most areas. But when we were in our base camp, a deep fox hole was the best place to be.

The constant raids were nerve-wracking to us all. To improve morale, our commanding officer had the troops fill sand bags and place them in rows on the sloping side of a steep hill, to be used as seats. A "stage" and a screen were set up at the bottom, and we occasionally saw a movie.

In Society was the name of one film. I'll never forget it, though I never watched it. For four or five nights in a row we gathered at that hill to watch the movie. As it became dark enough to run the film, the air raid sirens sounded "Condition Red". The Japs were coming!

We took cover—every time—and never saw the movie.

Jo Jo and the Giant Tarantula

◆

Our Saipan base camp had eight-man canvas tents mounted on elevated wood floors. Every tent contained two canvas and wood folding cots on each of its four sides. My cot was next to the doorway, its canvas flap open anytime there wasn't a heavy downpour of tropical rain.

Every time we returned to camp from a combat patrol, we located and carried a huge stalk of bananas back with us. After eating the ripe ones, we hung the green bananas high up on the tent's center pole. The first Marine who got up in the morning had his choice of the bananas that had ripened overnight.

Sometimes there was a living guest in the stalk of bananas!

One night I awakened to see a huge tarantula spider on my mosquito netting, silhouetted against the sky. I could not tell whether it was on the outside, or inside.

I called to a buddy, "Maitland, are you awake?"

"No! Be quiet."

I said, "There's a giant spider on my mosquito net. Get your helmet liner and help me get rid of it."

He did. But he didn't bother to see which side of the net the spider was on. He slammed his helmet liner down, over the spider and onto my bare chest! Thankfully, the spider was on the outside of the netting. I pushed upward on each side of his helmet liner, and the tarantula was captured.

Wrapping the spider inside the mosquito net, we carried it outside and dumped it onto the moonlit, hard-packed ground.

Jo Jo, our company's monkey mascot (released from a shell-destroyed pet shop in Garapan, Saipan's capitol) had been alerted by our activities. He grabbed the tarantula as it tried to scurry away.

Then we watched as Jo Jo removed each of the spider's eight hairy legs, discarded them, and *ate* the legless tarantula like a hungry man would devour a large, juicy hamburger!

Jo Jo eating his tarantula treat

A Huge Bowl of Jello

If you thought I was shook up by my episode with Jo Jo and the tarantula, you would be wrong. The real shake-up came a few nights later.

The six of us were sound asleep when Mother Nature shook us awake. Literally!

Our tent began to move. Up and down. The floor was bouncing as though some huge monsters were wrestling beneath it.

The cots we had been sleeping on became like bucking broncos.

A movie showing six scantily-clad Marines just trying to stand up would have won an Oscar. Showing us attempting to walk would have won another.

Saipan was experiencing a major earthquake!

Fortunately, the quake did not last long.

Later, when asked to describe the event, I replied, "It was similar to what I believe one might expect when trying to walk on a huge bowl of wiggling Jello!"

When I attempted to take a step, the earth would either come up to meet my foot, or drop away. We had no control and the occurrence was unique for all of us. None of us had ever experienced anything more severe than an earth tremor before.

We thought Saipan was about to sink into the Pacific Ocean!

It was far more preferable to be awakened by the bugler.

Combat Swimming with Sharks

◆

One evening in our base camp tent a group of us, all Marines, were chatting when Private Bantiah entered and said, "There is an interesting new notice on the company's bulletin board. They're asking for a few Marine volunteers."

Bantiah's announcement was received by "hoots and hollers." It just wasn't the Marine Corps way to volunteer—for anything.

Nevertheless, three or four of us got up and went to investigate.

The notice said U. S. Navy Warrant Officer Archer would visit 3rd Battalion, 6th Regiment, 2nd Marine Division at 1300 hours (1:00 p.m.) the following day. Experienced swimmers, willing to undergo strenuous testing, were urged to volunteer for intensive, advanced training to become Combat Swimming Instructors.

I decided to volunteer though I didn't anticipate any possibility of being selected. However, it could be a welcome change to our regular schedule.

I was present when Warrant Officer Archer arrived, and I wasn't alone. More than one hundred Marines gathered to learn about the need for swimming instructors. Some of the Marines had worked as professional lifeguards on American beaches and for swimming pools at prestigious resort hotels. They had considerable experience, some even in the oceans. Most of the prospective instructors were also larger and stronger—much stronger—than I.

Warrant Officer Archer introduced himself as being in charge of U. S. Navy swimming in the Pacific Theater. He knew we had all demonstrated swimming ability before completing USMC boot camp but said he planned to select ten Marines for extreme testing. Their military training together with combat swimming experience was expected to be of great value in future clandestine operations against the Japanese.

I realized I had little chance of being among the ten Marines selected but I have always been a bit stubborn and prided myself on not quitting anything I started. I would just do my very best and await Warrant Officer Archer's interview, and his decision.

When asked about my swimming background, I acknowledged it as being entirely recreational and was limited primarily to swimming in Idaho's canals and the Snake River.

Warrant Officer Archer asked if I had any health problems in my background, including claustrophobia, how much alcohol did I usually consume and was I a user of tobacco in any form.

When I replied I'd never used alcohol, tobacco, or even caffeine, he seemed noticeably interested.

Upon conclusion of interviews, ten Marines were selected to undergo very strenuous swim and stress testing. I was one of the ten! Amazing!

Our group was detached from regular duties and was transported to beautiful Magicienne Bay on the south end of Saipan. Most of the bay was protected by a large, colorful coral reef. The beautiful, clear water was shallow near the white sand beach but there were places just inside the reef where depths were in excess of thirty feet. And there were many fish, including barracuda, several species of rays, and a variety of sharks.

Tall, majestic palm trees towered above giant green ferns along picture-perfect beaches.

There, the ten of us were assigned to U.S. Navy Swim Instructors, five of them.

With two Marines and one Navy instructor in each eight-man black neoprene raft, five rafts were rowed across the bay, lifted over the coral reef and into the ocean. And we didn't stop there.

When we were far out in the ocean, approximately one mile from the bay, each pair of Marines was ordered, at intervals, to swim ashore.

None of us had any problem with that initial test.

Next, in the deepest waters of the bay, we were each required to swim a certain distance using the Australian crawl, backstroke, side stroke, and breast stroke. Every one of us passed that test too. Floating (remaining in one spot) for a full ten minutes proved more problematic for two Marines. They were "excused" and returned to camp. Then eight of us were ordered to swim as far as we could under water. Upon completing that swim we were to remain under water as long as possible before surfacing! (It is easier to hold your breath when you are not moving.)

That test was a feat I had practiced many times with competitive boyhood friends in a Rigby, Idaho canal. Five more Marines were excused and returned to regular duty, though they were told they may be re-called if needed.

Amazingly, I was one of the three finalists. Warrant Officer Archer congratulated us, and then informed everyone that Don Jardine was number one on the underwater test, setting a new record for time underwater! Then he asked how I was able to remain under water so long, without panic.

Frankly, I had learned a lot by competing with my Idaho friends and knew that panic was a state of mind. There were many times I had nearly reached the panic stage where I felt I had to reach the surface and fill my lungs with delicious fresh air. But then, by talking myself into being calm, I'd find a reserve of air in my lungs and would force myself to remain below the water's surface for additional seconds beyond what I had considered my absolute limit.

I didn't describe that to Warrant Officer Archer. I just replied, "I guess it's because I don't drink, smoke, or kiss girls." That last item would perhaps be untrue except for the total unavailability of females on Saipan. Regardless, my explanation was accepted. Combat swimming instruction would begin at dawn the next day and would continue for nine consecutive days, excepting Sunday.

A large tent with a wooden floor had been constructed for the three of us. It was only 40 or 50 feet back from the water's edge on a white sand beach and under picture-perfect palm trees. Truly idyllic.

Newspaper clipping: "Instructor on Saipan"

Instructor on Saipan

Marine Pvt. Donald Jardine, grandson of Josiah Godfrey of 555 D street, Idaho Falls, is now a combat swimming instructor on Saipan, according to his grandfather.

Private Jardine became an instructor after he had recovered from wounds received during the invasion of Saipan. He received shrapnel wounds in the legs from a mortar and has since spent considerable time in a hospital.

His parents, Mr. and Mrs. L. H. Jardine, have received his purple heart award. The 18 year old marine has been in the service for 15 months. He was a carrier of The Post-Register in Rigby for one year while going to junior high school.

The extra Navy swimming instructors returned to their ship in Tanapag Harbor, while two remained with us and put us through several difficult and sometimes hazardous experiences. Then they too left us.

We were now certified Combat Swimming Instructors.

From our tent we easily could see Tinian Island, only three miles to our south, as we taught large groups of Marines.

One inconvenience was attributable to that seemingly perfect location. We were at the south end of the only operative airfield on Saipan (Aslito Airfield) and it was a major target for enemy aircraft. Almost every night we were awakened by loud sirens announcing the approach of Japanese bombers. That noise was soon added to by our anti-aircraft guns and the crump, crump, crump of Japanese bombs falling nearby.

Quite regularly, practically every third day, the air raid sirens interrupted us, warning of approaching enemy fighter planes, usually while we were in the black rubber rafts we used while teaching. We would row ashore as quickly as possible and find concealment under vegetation (there were no air raid shelters available) and wait out the air strikes. Those raids didn't last long due to fuel limitations.

Sometimes it was quite a show because our P-47s (Thunderbolts) and P-38s (twin-boomed Lightnings) engaged the Japanese planes overhead. It was far more exciting than any football or basketball game. And it was real!

As swimming instructors, our jobs were repetitive, teaching group after group of Marines the same lessons. The routine became boring. Our only recreation came at the end of each day's teaching. Then the three of us would don a "face plate" (face mask) and swim fins for shell hunting excursions, always together. We'd cross the large coral reef and dive in deep water to extract specific types of shells from the colorful coral formations. They were valued more than money, or as money, by the natives.

We never swam in or near the bay without being in close proximity to sharks. Many sharks. Large sharks—up to 10 feet long!

Natives told us we were relatively safe, but to watch out for barracuda. Those torpedo-like fish, each one sporting a large mouth with rows of needle-like teeth, often sped past us, dashing in to get pieces of marine matter that had been dislodged as we used our K-bar knives to dig out desired shells.

One day, on the ocean side of the reef, I was covered by the shadow of some large thing above me, moving slowly toward my nearest swimming companion. He was less than twenty feet beyond me when the object moved between us. I quickly recognized it as a midget Japanese submarine like those used by the enemy during their attack on Pearl Harbor!

Wrong! It slowly turned and my companion and I, each of us less than ten feet away from the object, aged immediately. It was a great white shark more than sixteen feet long and far bigger around than a fifty gallon drum!

As unobtrusively as possible, we moved alongside the reef and clambered over the coral, into the welcome, relative security of the bay.

The greatest recorded depth of any ocean on earth is the Mariana Trough. Its proximity to Saipan probably explains, as the natives told us, why great white sharks and other large sharks are not uncommon there.

Instructing Marines in combat swimming was my most enjoyable service in the Marine Corps. I sincerely wish I could share with you the beauties of a complete world in the depths of tropic waters; thousands of fish varying in size, shape, patterns, colors, and even behaviors; brilliant colors of coral, etc.

We would have been delighted to have scuba gear but that was not available. We had to hold our breath to view the fantastic beauties that, even now, most people have no idea exist.

I spent approximately one hundred days in that tropical underwater heaven, and I have always remembered it as one of the highlights of my life—the world's largest and most beautiful aquarium.

With sharks.

Close encounter with the great white shark

548113
DGW-rdc
IN REPLYING ADDRESS
COMMANDANT OF THE MARINE CORPS
WASHINGTON 25, D. C.
AND REFER TO

SERIAL

HEADQUARTERS U. S. MARINE CORPS
WASHINGTON

10 October 1946.

TO WHOM IT MAY CONCERN.

The records of this office show that Donald LeRoy JARDINE, 548113, while attached and serving with the Second Marine Division was designated a Qualified Combat Swimming Instructor.

E. J. COSTELLO,
Captain, U. S. Marine Corps.

3ND-NRMC-42

IN REPLYING ADDRESS
COMMANDANT OF THE MARINE CORPS
WASHINGTON 25, D. C.
AND REFER TO
DGK-1505-kfb
548113

DEPARTMENT OF THE NAVY
HEADQUARTERS UNITED STATES MARINE CORPS
DISCHARGED PERSONNEL UNIT, RECORDS SERVICE SECTION
U. S. NAVAL RECORDS MANAGEMENT CENTER
GARDEN CITY, NEW YORK

4 May 1951

Mr. Donald LeRoy Jardine
c/o Juab H. S. Art Department
Nephi, Utah

TO WHOM IT MAY CONCERN

The records of this office show that Donald LeRoy JARDINE, 548113, qualified as a Combat Swimming Instructor on 23 December 1944, and there is no record of this qualification being revoked prior to his discharge on 25 January 1946.

R. G. WILSON
First Lieutenant, U. S. Marine Corps
Head, Discharged Personnel Unit, Records Service Section
By direction of the Commandant of the Marine Corps

Swimming Instructor Certificates issued by Marine Corps and by Navy

Same Day, Same Month, Different Year

On December 7, 1944, the three-year anniversary of the bombing of Pearl Harbor, my battalion was ordered to maneuver on the north end of Saipan. The three rifle companies of 3rd Battalion, 6th Regiment, 2nd Marine Division (minus one platoon from each that were on regular combat patrol rotation in the jungles) were ordered to "saddle up."

We went to the north end of Saipan, not to the jungles, but instead to a relatively open area in which the Japanese had been building a landing strip prior to our invasion of Saipan. (The nearby heavy jungles were our usual hunting ground for armed Japanese army holdouts.)

As usual, it was a sweltering hot, clear day. My company ("I" Company) and "K" Company clambered out of trucks and up the side of a mountain overlooking the former enemy airport and a wide expanse of the Pacific Ocean.

At a signal from a Marine officer, we sat on the ground and waited to observe "L" Company go through maneuvers under simulated combat conditions. Each of the two observing companies would be taking a turn completing a similar but different problem, so we watched intently as "L" Company completed its assignment very realistically and quite successfully. There had been everything from bazookas to machine guns, flame throwers, cannons, mortars, rifle and hand grenades, tanks, half-tracks, and more.

Two hundred B-29's left Saipan to bomb Tokyo that day, the largest B-29 raid on Japan up until that time. As we sat and watched from the mountainside, the bombers all passed very low over us, en route to drop tons of bombs on the enemy homeland. We were feeling good and were giving hopeful estimates as to how soon we would win the war.

"L" Company finished its exercise, assembled into route march order, and started marching toward our observation point. We were next and I was near the head of the column as my company marched toward "L" Company on the glaring white coral road, determined to improve upon the tactics we had just seen.

As we marched eastward and "L" Company approached us, three P-47 fighters zoomed in formation toward us, each on the tail of the other. They were at very low altitude. We cheered, believing they would be giving us air support.

We were quickly proved wrong by the sudden staccato of machine guns firing. If these were our planes, they weren't using very good marksmanship! Bullets were kicking up a cloud of dust and the ricocheting bullets whined off rocks all around. Plane number two, in the center, was firing at plane number one! Impossible! Then the lead plane began trailing heavy black smoke. It had been hit! Madness!

I saw the center plane turn. There was a big red spot on its wing! It was a Jap Zero! The plane in the lead was ours, a P-47, and so was the last plane. The last plane was unable to fire at the Zero because bullets missing the Zero would hit the lead P-47

With all its machine guns still firing, the Zero headed toward our two companies of Marines.

Clouds of dust popped from the white coral road as the fighter's bullets churned a wide and fast-moving trail headed directly toward us.

We jumped off both sides of the coral road into the sparse, low shrubbery as dust from the spraying bullets raced toward us. We lay prone on the ground, hugging it and praying. This could be our last minute alive!

Then, over the terrifying sounds of the Jap Zero and its death-spouting machine guns came another roaring sound. Diving directly down from Heaven was a U.S. Air Force P-38 twin-boomed fighter plane, its guns blazing. They struck their target, hitting the Zero and stopping the trail of deadly bullets only a few yards from us.

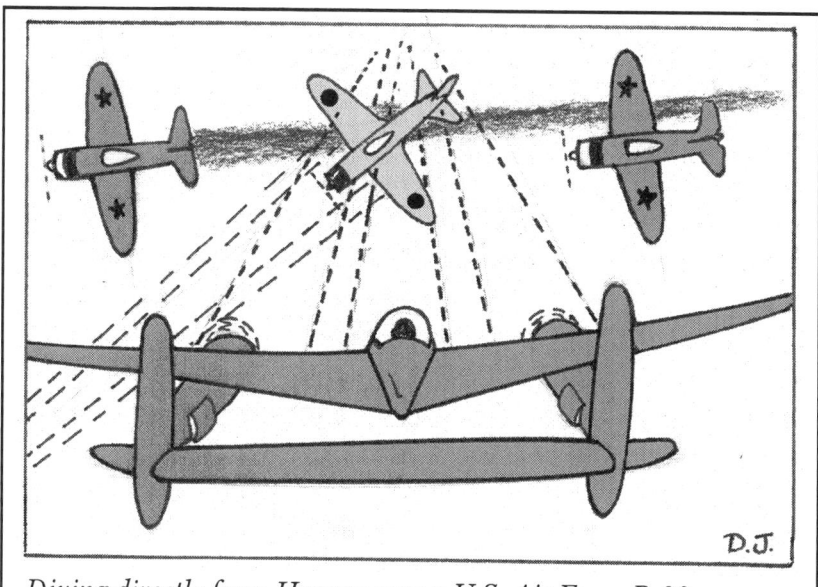

Diving directly from Heaven was a U.S. Air Force P-38 twin-boomed fighter plane, its guns blazing.

The Zero burst into flames. Trailing thick black smoke, it barrel-rolled out of control and crashed into the ocean no more than 800 yards away.

More dramatic than a Hollywood movie, this occurred so rapidly I didn't see what happened to the damaged P-47, but was later told that it and its companion flew on toward the Aslito Airfield on the south end of Saipan. Presumably, the victorious P-38 did the same.

I wish I could have met and thanked the P-38's pilot. He saved many lives—including mine.

Writing this account takes far more time than the action itself.

That third anniversary of the Japanese sneak attack on Pearl Harbor is a day I'll never forget. I immediately determined to celebrate my survival every year on that date for the rest of my life. I have and I will!

Pinup Art

Except for rare packages from home, which almost always were received in a deplorable condition, we had no source for "treats" like chips, candy bars, gum, ice cream, sodas, etc. But those things were usually available, for sale, in ships' stores.

Overseas, we were paid but never saw the money. Our $50.00 per month was recorded "on the books," never reaching our pockets. Therefore, going aboard a ship, any ship, was frustrating.

On one ship a buddy wore a dungaree jacket upon which, at his request, I had drawn a pretty girl. It caught the attention of several

Pinup girl

envious Navy men who inquired as to how he had obtained such fine art.

It was a solution to our penniless situation. I began doing drawings on sailors' jackets, for $5.00 each. Naval officers would not permit their men to dictate a lack of apparel, but "skimpy" was allowed.

Here are some drawings similar to those that proved most popular, and that enabled me (and more buddies than I knew I had) to patronize ships' stores.

All of my drawings, sad to say, were done without models!

Pinup girl

Pinup girl

B-29 Bomber Missing over Japan

On Saipan, I received a letter from a former Rigby schools classmate, stained with tears.

She had heard I was serving in the South Pacific as a Marine, and hoped I was in the Marianas. Because of censorship, people back home never knew exactly where I was. Her husband, pilot of a B-29 Super Fortress Bomber, flying missions from Saipan to Japan, had just been listed as missing in action. His plane had not returned from a bombing raid on Tokyo and she was desperate for additional information. She wondered if I could get to Aslito Airfield on Saipan and obtain first-hand information from members of her husband's squadron.

If I could get any information it wouldn't be possible for me to share it with her, due to censorship, but I could at least let her know whether or not I had learned anything by writing that "our friends have not yet supplied the information we asked for." My friend would understand and know I had at least tried.

My battalion was always on call, so getting permission to be off base was difficult and rarely obtained. However, when I had the Company Commander read my friend's pathetic letter, he granted a six-hour pass on a Saturday (from 12:00 noon until 6:00 p.m.).

Hitching a ride from base camp near the center of Saipan to Aslito Airfield, located on the south end of the island, several miles away, was simple. Finding the squadron leader of the missing B-29 took more time. Even so, I did locate him and asked for any information he had about my friend's husband. He read her letter and with tears on his cheeks he said, "That pilot is my best friend, but I have no information to give you. Nobody on that raid saw his ship go down, nobody saw an explosion or a trail of smoke, and no parachutes were sighted. We can only hope that the crew was able to parachute to 'safety,' and are now prisoners of war in Japan."

He told me nobody had heard anything from the missing plane's radio...but there was a lot of flak on that raid. It was for that reason—and to preclude attacks by Japanese fighter planes—that his squadron was flying high above a heavy blanket of clouds. Unable to descend below those clouds, they dropped their bomb loads indiscriminately, not being able to see their assigned targets, and then returned to Saipan. Nobody had any information about the missing B-29.

I was introduced to several flight crews and made instant friends. The airmen had many questions about ground, face-to-face combat and after I'd shared stories about some combat patrols, they unanimously agreed they preferred making bombing raids.

After I expressed my heartfelt interest in flying and told about my unsuccessful attempt to enlist in the Air Corps pilot training (due to being underage), they invited me to accompany them on a raid to Japan! I eagerly accepted, wondering how I'd be able to get another short leave from base camp, especially for the recommended 24 hours to allow for possible weather delays.

Because my platoon had just completed a full week of combat patrols and was scheduled for two weeks of guard duty, work details, training, inspections, etc., before our next combat patrol, I was granted a 12-hour pass!

Delighted that the necessary arrangements had been made, I hitchhiked back to Aslito Airfield early on the appointed day. My new Air Force friends greeted me with the information, "We're bombing Kobe, Japan today."

Takeoff time was an hour away so preparations for a special picnic were being made to enjoy on our return flight.

I was taken on a tour of the bomber we'd fly in. It was huge! It even had a stainless steel "tunnel," a tube large enough for a man to easily slide through when moving from one end (front to back) to the other.

My new friends even showed how the remotely controlled machine guns were fired.

The bomb bay was loaded with large bombs, many of which were decorated with clever things the Japanese would never read (unless the bomb was a dud), for example: "Hirohito, get a bang out of this!"

Takeoff time came...and passed, due to weather over the target.

The second takeoff time came...and passed. The weather had worsened. When the third takeoff time was announced, I quickly and sadly determined that I was unable to go on the raid and return to camp without being A.W.O.L (absent without official leave). Regretfully, I thanked the crew for doing their best to have me fly with them and I hitchhiked back to base camp. It was a major disappointment. I had so looked forward to what I knew would be the adventure of a lifetime.

No word from American or Japanese sources was ever received about my friend's husband, his plane, or crew. It remains a mystery.

After World War II

On a Ship to Japan

♦

Saipan, the Mariana Island I had called home for more than a year, was fading in the distance astern as the evening sun dropped toward the western horizon ahead. We (3rd Battalion, 6th Regiment, 2nd Marine Division) were aboard a troop ship headed for occupation duty in the city of Nagasaki, the recently destroyed target of our second atomic bomb.

The war was over.

Although hostilities had ceased, most of us were uneasy as it became dark because there were lights all over the ship. Heretofore, absolutely no light had ever been permitted where it might be seen by an enemy submarine, ship, or airplane. There had always been complete blackouts to avoid detection by the enemy. We had never before seen a ship with its lights on. Now we could occasionally see ships in the distance lighted up like Christmas trees! It was a wonderful new experience.

The war really was over!

When the Land of the Rising Sun was finally sighted, it was a sliver of blue-gray in the far distance, seemingly floating on the ocean surface. Most of the Marines aboard crowded the rails to watch as we gradually approached the homeland of Japanese soldiers we had dispatched elsewhere.

We had reservations about going ashore, not knowing how we'd be received. However, we were assured that the Japanese people, military and civilians, would heed instructions from their esteemed god-Emperor, who had warned that no attack upon the occupying forces would be tolerated.

Gradually objects in the distance became identifiable. Between our ship and the mainland were a number of tiny islands and dozens of small craft, all flying the Japanese flag. Most of the boats were old fishing craft with crews of two to ten men. They all stood on deck watching us.

Our ship slowed considerably as it threaded its way between the uncharted islands, most of which were too small for occupancy.

When we were within a half mile of land and of the waterway leading to Nagasaki's harbor, the ship stopped and dropped anchor. Jap officials had warned we could go no farther due to a large, deadly minefield that was navigable only by a Japanese Naval Pilot.

It was more than a day later when the Jap pilot boat pulled alongside. We took the pilot aboard, then weighed anchor for transit through the dangerous enemy mines.

As we neared the mouth of the waterway leading to Nagasaki, we saw long white bundles of rope-tied canvas floating past us—several of them. The Jap pilot explained that they were bodies. Their families, unable to afford the cost of a traditional cremation, had dumped them into canals at high tide and as waters receded at low tide they were carried out to sea.

Those bodies were people of all ages who were terminally injured by radiation from the atomic bomb. They had finally succumbed. Some bomb victims survived longer before passing away, but there were far fewer white bundles floating out to sea by the time we left Nagasaki four months later.

Seeing so many corpses—some much smaller than others—heightened our awareness of the personal loss suffered by survivors of the A-bomb's blast. Countless families who had lost male military members in the war were now losing their children, women, parents, and grandparents.

Canal in Nagasaki at low tide. At night, during high tide, victims of the atomic bomb were placed in this canal, to be carried out to sea as the tide went out.

Safely through the minefield, our ship made its way inland, toward what little remained of Nagasaki. Most of the buildings were destroyed and it is estimated that 40,000 to 70,000 persons died within the first few months after the bomb was dropped.

As some Marines read old magazines, played cards, or napped, I stood at the rail taking in fascinating sights. Very foreign-looking buildings lined both sides of the waterway.

Japanese civilians, walking along a pathway of stones, stopped to stare at us. We stared back, enthralled by their colorful kimonos, *geta-* (wooden) and *zori-* (straw) clad feet, and other traditional clothing. I couldn't move my eyes fast enough to see all the historic, awesome sights surrounding us. I was anxious to memorize everything I saw and wished I could share those fascinating sights with family and friends. Oh for a camera (and USMC permission to own and use one)!

Join the Marines and see the world!

Shrines like this remained along a walkway we followed when hiking around and through the rubble of Nagasaki.

In Japan: Nagasaki after the A-Bomb

The waterway ended at Nagasaki's harbor. We disembarked and marched to a four-story office building just south of the area destroyed by the atomic bomb. This building reportedly had housed offices for the Mitsubishi ship building company, and was within easy walking distance of what *little* remained of a Nagasaki business district.

A large stone-lined canal ran parallel to the front of our building, and a small footbridge enabled pedestrians and cyclists to cross over. A small *Kempetai* (Japanese Police) guard shack was located at one end and civilians considered "suspicious" were sometimes snatched inside.

Rumors said the *Kempetai* interrogated persons suspected of black-marketing and other serious crimes. If guilt was determined by the Jap police, they often meted out punishment on the spot! Our Military Police soon corrected that situation.

All civilians were desperately afraid of their police. Frankly, it was pathetic to watch them scurry across the footbridge, passing the guard shack with eyes averted and in obvious fear.

When we first arrived at the Mitsubishi Building, there were perhaps twenty to thirty women washing clothes in the canal not more than twenty feet from the building's main entrance. Ranging in age from about sixteen or seventeen to probably fifty or so, every one was nude from the waist up. Modesty was not part of the Japanese vocabulary, up to that time. For young men who hadn't seen a woman for many months, let alone women so well-endowed, it was cause for hundreds of Marines to hoot, whistle, shout, etc. Their reactions were quickly and correctly interpreted by the women, who from then on all wore concealing clothing.

Speaking of clothing, the Marines were anxious to acquire and send all kinds of Japanese souvenirs to their families in the States. Flags were "old hat" to most of us, but colorful kimonos and sashes were highly prized, and available. Some were purchased with the Japanese-engraved, U.S.-government-printed "script" we had been issued (and which Marines called fake money). Most, however, were obtained by trading: soap, chocolate, tobacco, etc. That was in September or early October. Later, when it began to get cold, the Japanese were often attempting to buy back clothing they had sold or traded to Marines. But those items had already been sent stateside.

Small children quickly learned we were not to be feared—and that we were a good source of candy, gum, soap and cigarettes for adults in their family. The generosity of Marines knew no bounds.

We saw many children carrying a baby brother or sister in a sling behind their back. In fact, I was amazed to see them playing games and running as fast as they could with the baby's head flopping like crazy! I never did learn whether the baby was asleep or unconscious, but they kept their eyes closed and didn't cry!

Japanese girl, atomic bomb survivor, playing baseball with a baby on her back

Another interesting thing was juggling. I believe every elementary school age child could juggle three (sometimes four) balls or bean bags effortlessly. Juggling seemed as popular with those children as marbles and jacks were with American kids.

There were no motor vehicles in Nagasaki, but they did have rickshaws.

Rickshaws in Japan

Our "passes" were infrequent and usually from noon until 6:00 p.m.

During one "pass," my buddy—Joseph P. Frankowski from New York—and I spotted a photographer's shop in the Mariamamachi District, located behind a hill which had provided protection from the exploding atomic bomb. I suggested we have a souvenir photograph taken together.

"Why?" Frank asked. "We could have a photo taken in Los Angeles, Chicago or New York and say it was taken in Japan. Nobody would know the difference."

"Not so!" I said.

Spotting two young Japanese men walking by, I approached them and, in my limited Japanese, asked them to follow us. We all went into the photographer's shop and had a photo taken. It turned out quite well. Many people have seen it and none have doubted it was taken in Japan.

Joseph P. Frankowski (left) and Don Jardine, in the Mariamamachi District of Nagasaki, with two young Japanese men

I agreed with the estimate that up to nine-tenths of Nagasaki was destroyed by the atomic bomb. Piles of rubble and a few steel frames of buildings remained. Radiation still affected many people but there were attempts by some survivors to restore business as usual. My "shopping" enabled me to buy or trade for an opium pipe in a wooden case and some chopsticks to send stateside as gifts. But make no mistake, when I say businesses, there were very few and they had extremely limited and simple, inexpensive items to sell or trade.

Japanese family business

I was fortunate in locating a unique item I kept as my personal souvenir. It is a tapestry depicting flags of the League of Nations, which preceded the current United Nations. I was told it took two women a full year to produce. It still remains in my art collection.

Detail from League of Nations tapestry

The point of the atomic bomb's detonation (well above the ground's surface) was easy to determine, although there was no crater. Practically everything that remained after the explosion leaned away from the blast.

Metal infrastructure leans away from the atomic explosion.

Heavy steel beams of large buildings sagged like wet spaghetti from the bomb's intense heat. And even they were usually few and far between. Most buildings, and their contents, had simply disappeared, leaving empty cement floors.

Steel drapes like wet spaghetti from the bomb's intense heat.

Remains of Catholic Church doorway in Nagasaki after the atomic bomb blast

A cement-lined canal that wound its way through what had been a large city was almost dry. An occasional puddle of stagnant water or drying mud contained bits of wood, brick, cloth, glass, paper, and other debris.

Before the atomic bomb exploded, this Nagasaki canal was surrounded by large buildings.

Even those of us who knew that baseball is Japan's favorite sport were nevertheless intrigued by a baseball diamond near the center of the A-bomb area. There was no doubt what it was, but there was no stadium from which spectators had watched the games. It had disappeared!

I walked the sidewalk shown on the right side of the photo many times. This was at the extreme eastern edge of Nagasaki's bomb blast area. Ahead lay a few unharmed businesses shielded from the explosion by a small hill.

We never saw many Japanese civilians. Those who still remained in the area and had a residence hardly ever left it. But we did notice that men and their wives seldom walked side-by-side. The woman walked several paces behind her husband. When we asked about that unusual situation, it was explained that Japanese women showed respect for their husband by avoiding stepping on his shadow—whether or not a shadow existed. The distance between husband and wife indicated her degree of respect, how "tall" she considered him to be.

I sketched this typical building while I was serving in Nagasaki after the atomic bomb.

Going to the restroom in Nagasaki was quite an experience. There were only a few, and all were located street-side, open in front, similar to American bus stops. A couple of boards extended from one end wall to the other, and appropriate holes (usually six to eight) had been cut to accommodate the users' needs. Men often urinated wherever and whenever Mother Nature dictated. Women used the "restrooms" (called *benjos*) and so did men whose bowels required it.

It was not uncommon to see Mr. Yamamoto seated next to Miss or Mrs. Shizowa, open to public view! No modesty.

Some Marines came back to our quarters with descriptive tales of visits to local bathhouses. There, Japanese men and women of all ages, including families, bathed together. Nude. No modesty.

Things changed rapidly after the Marines, and later the sailors, arrived. Their cheers and catcalls quickly changed ancient Japanese customs.

Japanese family moving their belongings in a handcart

Japanese woman carrying salvaged lumber

Inspecting a Japanese Freighter

◆

Established in our new quarters, we were given our first assignment. Every ship in the harbor was to be thoroughly searched.

I was ordered to inspect a medium-sized freighter. That was a fascinating experience for several reasons. The ship was quite dark below the main deck, so it was difficult to determine the contents of some boxes and sacks. And that was important because I was to look for weapons, ammunition, explosives, and other contraband. Determining that no Jap military personnel were aboard proved much easier.

The low overheads necessitated walking stooped over. Japs, being much shorter as a rule, didn't have that problem. The average adult Japanese was reportedly 5 feet 3 inches tall.

The tour of the ship was thorough and led (at my direction) by the very frightened ship's captain accompanying me. He was no doubt intimidated by my six-foot plus, uniformed frame. Also, I carried a .45 caliber semi-automatic pistol on my ammunition belt, which also contained a K-bar knife.

You have never seen anyone so eager to please nor so polite. Overly so! He even presented me with the ship's large flag, which I still have.

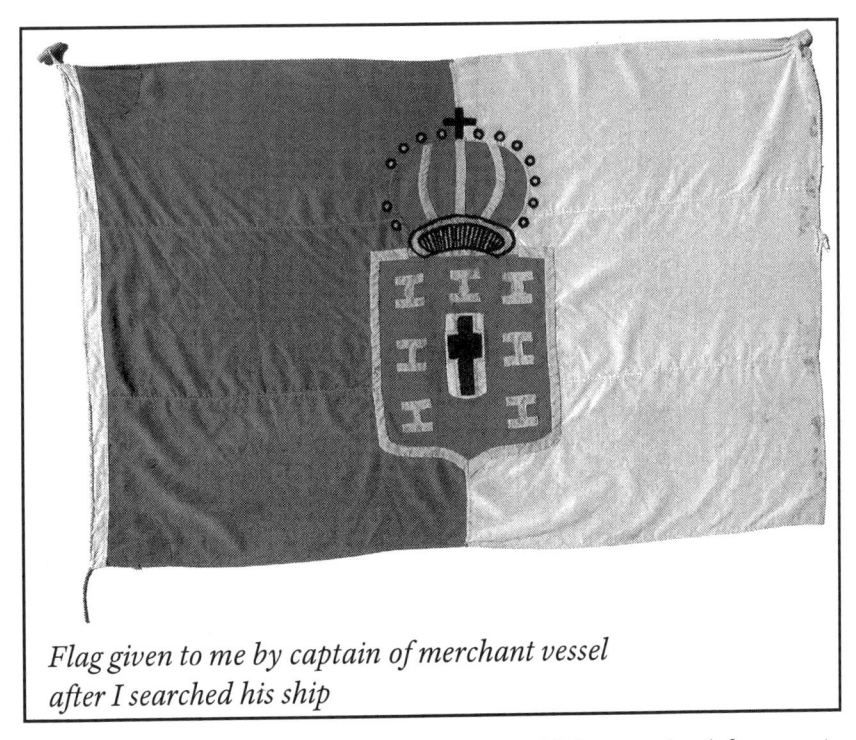

Flag given to me by captain of merchant vessel after I searched his ship

However, had I been smarter, I would have asked for a pair of binoculars instead—or also! They were large, expensive and had remarkable clarity at great distances. Japanese optics were highly regarded at that time. I have no doubt the ship's captain would have turned them over to me without hesitation.

A Hike through the Nagasaki Atomic Bomb Area

◆

We had been in Nagasaki less than 72 hours when I was summoned to the Commanding Officer's quarters. He asked if it was true that I could speak Japanese.

I replied, "No sir."

Then he said, "Several Marines have told me otherwise. Did you attend Japanese language school?"

"No sir."

"Then why do so many people tell me you are conversant in the Japanese language?"

I said, "Well sir, while my friends were playing poker, shooting craps and such, I spent that time studying the Japanese phrase books issued by the Corps. And on patrols, I was usually the one who tried to talk with Jap soldiers in caves, and talked with Japanese prisoners."

"Good! You're what we need. There are a couple more Marines that did the same thing—and I want the three of you beside me on a hike through the atomic bomb area, today!"

I was among those in the lead of our battalion as we hiked through the rubble of what had been the major Japanese city of Nagasaki.

We were reportedly the first Caucasians to walk through the rubble of that devastated city. It was quite a hike.

At every rest break, while others lay on the ground or sat on metal items that survived the atomic bomb's explosion, I took the opportunity to talk with Japanese civilians searching through the rubble of what had been their home, business, church, or school. One woman (*oksahn*) seemed impressed that I could converse, though slowly and with limited vocabulary, in her language. Before I had to leave she located a small decorated dish. It was the only thing I saw from the A-bomb area in one piece. She smiled as she offered it to me, saying, "*Dozo, tomodachi.*" (Here, friend.) It was a touching and memorable experience.

My habit of trying to talk to the Japanese probably saved me from the exposure to radiation which caused several Marines to

At a break during our hike through the atomic bomb area, some Marines sat on heavy machinery, suffering severe radiation burns.

suffer horrible, painful radiation burns and huge blisters. During a rest stop, while I interacted with Japanese, these men sat on drill presses and other metal objects that were extremely radioactive.

Three men from my company suffered severe radiation burns during that march. Their burns—large, ugly blisters and bright red skin—extended from the inside of one ankle through to the inside of their other ankle, as if they had sat on a red hot saddle.

Anything that touched them caused excruciating pain and there was the likelihood of their blisters bursting and skin peeling. Nothing had been applied to help alleviate their pain, nor would it be. Mother Nature would have to heal them. Medications of any kind were painfully intolerable.

They couldn't stand anything to touch the painful area and had to lay on their back nude, knees bent and legs wide apart, for nearly two weeks before they could be moved. They were then transported to a military hospital in the States. Their main concern was, would they ever be able to father children?

I contacted one of those Marines, Richard Oman of Chisolm, Minnesota, years later. He told me he and the other injured Marines were rated 100% disabled for the rest of their lives. He passed away not long after we talked. We had planned to get together, but never had the opportunity so I still have many unanswered questions.

A War Crime

On one occasion the commanding officer of our battalion ordered all occupants of the Mitsubishi Building to report topside. As we gathered on the flat roof, we were ordered to form ranks and stand at attention.

There was no explanation, but Marine officers, MP's and serious-looking Japanese officials, accompanied by a Japanese girl of perhaps ten to twelve years of age, passed along the ranks. The girl looked closely at every Marine and shook her head before proceeding.

We later learned that a Marine had handed the girl a can which she believed held food. (We all gave food items to hungry Jap kids.) She took the can home to her father. When he opened it, there was an explosion. The can contained an armed hand grenade!

By the time we reached Japan, many Marines had reached their emotional limits with the Japanese. They had been wounded (some several times) and seen their buddies maimed and killed. They had witnessed Saipan civilians committing suicide, often with infants in their arms and toddlers holding their hand, by leaping off high cliffs after Jap military told them lies about the Marines and what civilians could expect if captured: torture, rape, murder, etc.

As far as I know, the Marine who had given the grenade-loaded can was never identified or located. However, it was a frightening experience for every Marine because that little girl could have pointed at anyone and his fate would have been sealed!

Coming Home

♦

    After four months in Nagasaki, we departed for Sasebo via a narrow gauge Japanese train. We were a very happy battalion because the point system had been announced and it determined which Marines would return stateside first.

    As I remember, there was one point for each month served since enlisting, another point for each month overseas, five points for each campaign and five more points for every medal. My Purple Heart (I hadn't yet been awarded the second) pushed me into the stateside category. Less fortunate buddies remained in Japan another three months or so, but said they had a ball. They were bivouacked in small, private homes rented for them in Sasebo, and had young, healthy, attractive (reportedly), live-in maids who "provided all services."

    Getting to Sasebo was a unique experience to say the least. The train chugged through numerous tunnels and we were hardly able to see or breathe due to the heavy, black clouds of smoke from the laboring engine ahead. And train loads of very hostile Jap P.O.W. soldiers (back from captivity in Russia) passed us going in the direction from which we had come. I knew enough Japanese to wish I had a few grenades I could share with them, and it was probably just as well my buddies didn't understand what was being shouted at us.

    In Sasebo, those of us who were to board ship to return stateside were lined up in front of a huge Japanese warehouse.

Then, single file, we were ordered to run through the warehouse. We could grab one Japanese rifle (.25 or .31 caliber) and one sword. No time to examine or choose!

I got a fairly good .31 caliber rifle and a Samurai sword with a temporary handle and sheath, both of unstained wood.

A Samurai sword is often a Japanese family's most prized possession. Many have expensive handles and sheaths. Some are even adorned with precious stones. Mine may have been that type—wood replacing the expensive handle and sheath which would remain at home, under protection of the family, until the Jap soldier returned at war's end.

I sold that sword in 1993 at a garage sale in Golden Valley, Minnesota for two hundred dollars. It really had no value for me or my family.

Friends aboard ship, en route home, gave me a Japanese sword (really an authentic U.S. Civil War sword and metal scabbard), plus two Japanese rifles, in exchange for drawings I did on their combat jackets. I gave a rifle to my dad and to each of my two brothers for use in Utah's good deer hunting.

During my entire service overseas, my mail had been censored. After the war ended and President Harry S. Truman announced the end of censorship, my mail was an exception! (Recipients of my letters told me so.) The Marine Corps did not want me to send drawings of the atomic bomb area to the states.

Every Marine boarding the States-bound ship was issued a waterproof packet of official United States Marine Corps photographs of the campaigns we had participated in and of the Nagasaki atomic bomb area. Several of those photographs are published in this book. An Okinawa packet was not issued.

Our departure from Sasebo was delayed by a huge storm. When we finally boarded a ship for the journey home, we were told the storm had passed. Not so! We had traveled perhaps one hundred miles in the Yellow Sea when the wind and waves carried our heavily loaded troop ship to amazing highs—then lows. Similar to going to the top of a mountain, then down into a deep valley, continuously and rapidly.

Sea Witch was the name of our ship and the captain's name was Davidowich. He reportedly sent S.O.S. signals during the worst of the storm and said, "I was a ship's captain in the Atlantic for seventeen years and I'll be damned if I know why they call this the Pacific!"

The storm was so severe the captain actually changed course at one time, headed out of the Yellow Sea and west toward Shanghai, China. But before we reached that port, radio information led him to resume our course. Crossing into the East China Sea, we were again caught up by the same storm before we reached the Pacific Ocean. News reports concerning this storm reported heavy damage to United States bases on Okinawa, including the destruction of hundreds of mail bags. We all wondered if some of those bags carried mail intended for our regiment.

We eventually passed north of the Hawaiian Islands. Then, due to fighting the storm, it was determined that we needed to refuel to reach San Diego. We turned back and went to Pearl Harbor. After refueling we resumed our trip, experiencing Christmas Eve, then Christmas Day, which turned into a second Christmas Eve followed by another Christmas Day! We had crossed the International Date Line.

Dozens of dolphins met our ship miles west of San Diego and escorted us into the harbor. Locals told us it was a very unusual occurrence.

Disembarking was interesting. A Red Cross unit greeted each of us as we stepped off the gangplank. I was handed a small box of milk and offered a donut. I declined the latter, saying, "No thanks. It would ruin the taste of the milk." I had drunk only one glass of fresh milk in nearly two years.

Bussed to Camp Pendleton, we had just settled in when a Marine entrepreneur came through our barracks with a cart loaded with small boxes of milk, oranges, and heads of lettuce. He knew what we'd want, and his cart rapidly emptied as his wallet filled.

I purchased milk and a head of lettuce. I ate the lettuce as if it were a large apple—the entire thing!

It was great to be home.

Had I felt I had been treated fairly, I probably would have stayed in the Marine Corps. Then I thought about my boot camp drill instructor who had been a Marine for more than eighteen years, and overseas most of that time. He was a corporal, the same rank I held when I received my honorable discharge—still a teenager!

That drill instructor, Corporal Smalley, probably knew the Corps better than General Vandegrift, Supreme Commander of the United States Marine Corps! He was muscular, intelligent, knowledgeable, and a truly dedicated career Marine. In any other branch of the military, I am confident he would have been commissioned and promoted to be a high-ranking officer. He preferred being a Marine.

Henry Patton and the Bataan Death March

Years after the war, I became a friend of Henry Patton. He was a frequent visitor to my Minneapolis home. During one of those visits, in 1986, I asked about his World War II experiences, especially the infamous Bataan Death March and his slavery as a Japanese prisoner of war. On the next page are the notes I wrote that evening:

Don L. Jardine, Ph.D. Combat Marine at Seventeen

HENRY PATTON
A Real American Hero

- ★ SHOT DOWN 3X in 1st 2 days of W.W. II !

- ★ 386 men in his outfit
  192 after 90 days
  75 died in Bataan Death March
  7 alive at War's end
  3 alive "Now" (1986)!

- ★ The ONLY survivor of 3 different patrols!

- ★ 18 months as a guerilla (Phillipines)

- ★ Taken prisoner. Prayed for will to resist...& retention of mental processes.

- ★ 41 days in solitary confinement with only 4 days of ANY light!

- ★ Christmas Eve 1943 spent in Old Spanish Prison — Bataan.

- ★ Weighed LESS than 80# in Phillipines. Weighed 67# at end of War in JAPAN !!!

Interview Notes by Don Jardine

My notes from an evening with my friend Henry Patton, Bataan Death March survivor

Thoughts on the Atomic Bombs

◆

I have frequently been asked to express my opinion concerning our nation's use of two atomic bombs. In fact, I wrote a magazine article about that subject soon after I returned home from Japan. Upon publication, readers of the magazine responded with opinions, positive and negative, in awesome numbers. They were quite evenly divided, fifty percent agreeing, fifty percent dissenting. My opinion is still in full agreement with dropping the bombs.

Consider this:

On Saipan, months before the bombs were dropped on Hiroshima and Nagasaki, our Marine company was ordered to gather around a large (approximately 4 feet by 10 feet) topographic map of Kyushu, Japan. We were told exactly where and how we would land as one spearhead for the invasion of Japan.

Even earlier, we had been briefed on a proposed invasion of Formosa (now called Taiwan). I was inexplicably fearful of participating in that operation, so it pleased me when the military leaders decided to bypass that island and invade the Japanese homeland instead.

Had we invaded Japan, the estimated casualties, Japanese and American, were astronomical—far more than those actually caused by our bombs. Knowing that, I firmly believe the development and use of atomic bombs saved countless lives,

Japanese as well as American. If we hadn't dropped those two bombs, the war would have lasted much longer. Many thousands of American military personnel would have died. In fact, some military leaders estimated there would have been 500,000 American casualties from an invasion of the Japanese homeland! Japanese casualties may have even exceeded that number.

Marines honor their fallen

There but for the grace of God go I

Back to School

♦

When I enlisted in the Marine Corps I said, "I'll never go through the door of another school." I was tired of studying. In the U.S. Marine Corps Boot Camp in San Diego, there were two illiterate hillbillies in my platoon. They were friendly, likeable fellows and we became close friends. When they offered to do my laundry if I'd read their letters from home and reply to them, I agreed. Both of them were being taught by the Marine Corps to read and write, so they remained in Boot Camp while the rest of us graduated and continued on to Camp Pendleton for further accelerated training.

Those two men helped me to realize the importance of education, so when I regained civilian status, I resumed going through school doors. Countless doors!

I graduated twice from Weber College in Ogden. That great junior college (now a four-year university) had conferred on me an associate of science degree *and* a certificate of completion in commercial art—both with honors.

My long-time desire to fly had been fulfilled when I learned that the G.I. Bill (which was paying my tuition at Weber College) allowed me to enroll in an aviation class. The class time earned physical science credits, and I also received ten hours of flight instruction. Great! That allowed me to train sufficiently to qualify for solo flight. Subsequently, Ogden Air Park rewarded me with ten hours free flight time for every flight student I referred to them.

To encourage Weber students to take flying lessons, I designed and had printed on bright yellow paper a hundred handbills. I posted them all over the campus and soon had a list of aspiring pilots eager to fly. This earned enough free flight hours for me to complete my private pilot license.

With my private license in hand, I was authorized to fly any single-engine aircraft, solo or with passengers. The passengers could share expenses, but I was not permitted to charge them for my services. That would have required a commercial pilot license and I was not prepared to make that career investment (competing with discharged Air Force pilots who had many hundreds of hours of flying experience).

Proud new pilot with Aeronca

I later enrolled at the University of Utah, majoring in secondary art education. Again, I graduated with honors. While there, I illustrated the university's literary magazine (*The Pen*),

My illustrations of fraternity and sorority houses at University of Utah

the university's yearbook (*The Utonian*), and was awarded a Gold Key for ink drawings of eighteen fraternity and sorority houses.

Many years later, while married and raising three children, working full-time at Art Instruction Schools, and teaching at the University of Minnesota, I went back to school to get a Ph.D. After years of studying in my "spare time," I earned my doctorate at age 49. That prompted my wife's aunt to state, "Carol's husband sure must be dumb if he can't get out of school at his age!"

I advise you, my reader, to do whatever you can to improve your education. Education is available everywhere in our great nation, even by Internet. Try it. You will like it.

Big Spence and the Wild Goose

◆

I was at the controls of the small two-seater Aeronca, gaining altitude as the Ogden Air Park receded behind us.

With several recently-added hours of flying instruction in my Pilot's Log Book, the flight tests for a private pilot's license were looming. Big Spence, a friend, veteran pilot and flight instructor with more than 8,000 hours flying time logged, had agreed to accompany me on a flight check to evaluate my flying performance. If his evaluation was good, I would certainly have no problems with any flight examiner's requirements.

We were headed for the designated flight practice area west of Ogden, over the shores of Great Salt Lake.

It was hunting season and I was maintaining a good altitude because hunters far below were shooting at ducks and geese flying nearer to the ground.

It was a new experience to see game birds fall *away* from us as buckshot from hunters' guns struck them and they fell to earth.

When a large flock of Canada geese appeared in our flight path, at our altitude, Spence said, "Let me have the controls Jardine."

He applied full throttle and the plane responded. Big Spence was intent upon overtaking a goose that was lagging slightly behind the flock.

As we approached the large bird, it glanced over its shoulder, realized we were about to overtake it and "poured on the coal." The bird flapped its wings furiously in a desperate attempt to stay ahead of our airplane's propeller.

Unsuccessfully!

Spence maneuvered the plane with precision, clipping the tail feathers of one frightened goose—and down it went.

And down *we* went!

The goose fell to the ground and Spence landed the plane right behind him.

Turning the controls back to me, Spence yelled, "Take over Jardine. I'll be right back!" Then he leaped from the still-moving airplane and ran past several startled hunters after his goose.

Surprise! The desperate bird was not seriously affected by the loss of a few tail feathers. He resumed flying!

Spence, undeterred, jumped back into the cockpit, took over the plane's controls again, and we chased the goose.

Prior events were repeated, but this time Spence made sure the plane's propeller clipped enough tail feathers to ensure that the bird, now falling to the ground a second time, would fly no more.

Again, Spence turned the plane's controls back to me as the landing gear touched the ground not far behind his goose.

The plane was still rolling as the big man again opened his door, jumped from the plane and chased his bird.

After running through tall marsh grasses, mud, water and swarms of mosquitoes, Spence finally captured his goose. He tucked it under his arm, opened the baggage compartment, shoved the panicked bird inside, slammed the door shut and resumed his seat inside the aircraft—exhausted.

The weary but desperate goose noisily flopped around in the baggage partition just behind the cockpit while Spence had me perform the maneuvers which would soon be required of me to pass the private pilot's flight tests: stall and recovery; 360 degree turn to the right (without loss of altitude); to the left 360 degrees (feeling the propeller's backwash); a pylon figure eight above two intersections below us (to determine proper corrections for wind drift); spin and recovery; an unexpected surprise when Spence cut the throttle and carefully observed my decisions just as would be required in an actual engine failure emergency, where to set the plane down, a safe gliding distance to avoid collision with objects on the ground, consideration of wind direction and effect, even my cutting the ignition as a precaution against fire, etc.

I was really put through a strict series of flight tests—with the Canada goose continually flapping its wings behind our seats.

When the tests were successfully completed, Spence had me fly back to the airport. After we landed, he climbed out of the plane saying over his shoulder, "Good job, Jardine. I'll take my goose inside. You clean the baggage compartment."

Sure!

I said, "Spence, that goose is not worth cleaning the baggage compartment. And it's your bird. You clean the compartment."

Inside the airport office, with several pilots seated around the pot bellied stove, Spence regaled them with details of our flight—and how he had caught *his* wild goose.

Oh how I wish I could share his storytelling with you. But even a movie would not substitute for his live performance.

Picture a large six-foot-four-inch man with snaggle teeth, glancing over his shoulder as the frightened goose had done, flapping his arms and large hands rapidly, imitating his bird and telling how he had leaped from the airplane, twice, to run after and capture his goose.

It was a hilariously funny comedy show that entertained his pilot audience as no non-live performance could have done.

Frankly, Spence really earned his goose dinner. Not just because he had succeeded in securing a tasty meal, but because he had a huge, difficult, dirty job cleaning the plane's baggage compartment.

I'll have a hamburger!

P.S. The check flight with Big Spence proved very helpful. I passed the private pilot flight examination the first time, and with a good score, despite previous flight distractions.

Soon after earning my private pilot's license, I realized that Spence, a veteran pilot, had taught valuable lessons my pilot friends did not even know about.

For example: You fly a low-powered "puddle jumper" into a box canyon. Ahead of you is a mountain you know rises in altitude faster than your plane can climb. You are unable to turn right or left because of the high ridges on either side. Landing is out of the question. When asked for a solution, most of my pilot friends replied that you quickly repeat the Lord's prayer, then crash!

Not if you had an outstanding instructor. Spence taught me to push the controls forward into a dive, to rapidly pick up speed to *loop* the airplane. Carefully judge the space you'll need to pull your plane into the loop, then, pull back on the controls until you are on the top of the loop. You will be upside down. Because few planes can fly very far inverted, you execute a wing-over and fly, right side up, back out of the canyon in the direction you entered.

Another helpful tip Spence taught me: As you approach a mountaintop, you can quickly ascertain whether you have sufficient altitude to clear the ridge. If you see increasing terrain beyond the mountain, you will be able to clear it. If you see less and less terrain beyond that mountain, you need more altitude before attempting to fly over it.

The Professor's Coat

◆

Our Weber College art class was seated and awaiting the arrival of Professor Farrell R. Collett. I believe he planned to arrive a few minutes late...for dramatic reasons.

Taking off his sport coat he threw it over a chair beside his desk. Then he stepped back, folded his arms and stood, apparently admiring his coat. Every student watched, wondering what this display was all about.

"Isn't that beautiful?" Professor Collett asked.

There was no response from any class member.

"Isn't that beautiful?" he repeated.

I'm sure most of us looked at Collett's coat and thought-- $29.95 at J.C. Penney, so what?

Hearing no response to his repeated question, Professor Collett pointed at a puzzled young man seated in front of him.

"Isn't that beautiful?" he asked a third time.

The student, aware that his reply was expected, said, "Yes sir. It is beautiful."

Professor Collett then pointed to a girl nearby and asked, "Isn't that beautiful?"

"Yes sir," the girl replied, "It is beautiful."

Turning back to the young man, he asked, "Why is it beautiful?"

The student was unable to reply.

"Well, what do you see?"

The young man replied, "A man's coat."

Professor Collett turned back to the girl and asked, "What do you see?"

Obviously aware that Professor Collett expected a more detailed answer, she replied, "I see a man's sport coat."

Then Professor Collett pointed to another student and asked, "What do you see?"

The student responded, "I too see a man's sport coat—a man's *brown* sport coat."

With a smile on his face, Professor Collett said, "I too see a man's brown sport coat. But let me tell you what else I see. I see a column fold, an inert fold, a drape fold and a spiral fold," as he pointed to each of them. "And I see several different colors and textures." He pointed them out. "Here is a light brown; here is a much darker brown; this is a cream color, and note the buttons. They are a reddish brown. This is a wool coat and it has a rough texture. Do you see how different the lining is—very smooth. And this label has both Gothic and Italic lettering. Also, there are all five values of light..." and he pointed out highlights, halftones, reflected lights, shadow edges, and cast shadows.

Professor Collett was teaching us to *see* what most people merely *look at*. And that, in my opinion, is one of the most valuable lessons anyone can learn. We all see things differently—or should I say—we all look at things differently.

Learning the principles and elements of art enables one to better appreciate *all* the Arts: music, dance, literature, drama, sculpture, poetry, painting, architecture, etc. It can truly enrich one's life, every day. But it takes a good art teacher to really open our eyes and enable us to see what others merely look at. Dr. Collett was such a teacher.

Mr. J. C. Penney Himself

In Ogden, Utah, while attending college, I learned about an employment opportunity at the large J. C. Penney store downtown. It sounded interesting. They needed someone to do "creative and attractive lettering on price cards, posters, banners and for displays. Portfolio required."

After assembling several examples of my lettering and artwork, I telephoned for an appointment.

Success! A Mrs. Blankenship, the store manager, would interview me personally.

The interview went well. I was hired on the spot, though I had to insist upon working around my own schedule. That proviso was accepted as long as all the assigned work could be completed as needed.

My work room was located on the lower floor—behind the ladies' dressing room. In fact, to get to the room I had to go *through* the ladies' dressing room. I had to ask a female employee to check occupancy for me to avoid embarrassing lady customers—or perhaps myself.

Several weeks after my employment as Show Card Artist, the Ogden City Chamber of Commerce announced a competition. Prizes, some quite substantial, would be awarded to participating stores in a variety of categories. Among them was: Most Attractive and Effective Window Displays.

When the J. C. Penney store won first place in that category, specific mention was made about the creative, artistic, beautiful and very legible lettering in every one of J. C. Penney's twenty-one window displays.

That award was well publicized. And so was an announcement by Mr. J. C. Penney. He would visit the Ogden store and accept the Chamber's award *personally*.

On the big day, I was asked to be at the store per Mr. Penney's specific request.

I was introduced to Mr. Penney, and he invited me to tour the store with him and Mrs. Blankenship. Examples of my lettering were not only in the display windows, but throughout the store. Mr. Penney exclaimed frequently about the displays and occasionally pointed out some of my lettering which he said he found especially attractive.

Upon completing our tour of all four floors in that huge store, Mr. Penney turned to me and said, "Congratulations young man. You do fine work. You have a job with J. C. Penney stores *anytime* you want one." Then he turned to the store manager and said, "Please make a note of that, Mrs. Blankenship."

It was a proud moment, but I don't know if the offer still holds, now that computers could replace me!

The Unforgettable Lecture

During more than ten years of college and university study, I listened to hundreds of lectures. Some were long, dry, boring, and even pathetic. Others were interesting, informative, brief, or amusing. They were on a wide variety of subjects and most of them were soon forgotten, or are remembered only vaguely. There was one exception. It stands out in my mind as being the most unforgettable lecture. Here is the story:

On the opening day of a new quarter, Professor Farrell R. Collett, head of the Art Department at Weber College in Ogden, Utah, greeted his students. Then he proceeded to describe an assignment which would be due the next time our class met. In essence, he said, "List ten items produced by mankind, yet that are in no way related to art." On the day the assignment was due and some time after all the students were seated, Professor Collett entered the room, picked up the top assignment sheet from the stack of papers which had been submitted and announced that he would lecture on the first item, describing its relationship to art. *Then* he looked at the list. The first item was cement.

Briefly, Professor Collett said, "Let's say the cement comes in paper bags. If there is a design on the bag, it was done by an artist. There is lettering on the bag. There are hundreds of variations of the 26 letters in the English alphabet. None grew on a tree, vine or bush. All were created by artists. In fact, the bag was designed by an artist. Where did the paper bag come from? A factory? Yes! Designed by an artist. There were machines in that factory, also designed by artists. How did the person who purchased the cement learn about that particular cement? By reading a newspaper or magazine advertisement? Probably. And that advertisement was created by an artist. And how was the cement transported to the purchaser? By truck, ship, plane or train? All designed by artists!"

With all due respect to Professor Collett, his lecture on cement became rather boring—as it dragged on for more than an hour. He related cement to art in a multitude of ways. But I am grateful for that lecture. Since then I have been increasingly appreciative of Farrell's intention. He wanted to impress his students with the vastness of art and the fact that there are innumerable vocational opportunities for people with good art training. It was an unforgettable lecture.

Too many people believe the artist is a person endowed with the innate ability to take a pencil or brush in hand and create something on paper or canvas that "looks just like a photograph." This is not true. The student who studies art as seriously as another would study medicine to become a doctor, or as one might study math to become a statistician, can probably attain sufficient proficiency to enable him to pursue art as a vocation.

Professor Collett shared the following philosophy with his students: "If one can earn a living doing that which he would ordinarily do for pleasure, he has found his true vocation." Art can be learned, and if a person enjoys art, he may well consider making it his life's work.

Dr. Collett and the Math Teacher

♦

One of the many things that made Dr. Farrell Collett's art classes so very interesting was his wealth of stories. True stories. One of my favorites was about when he was teaching art for Provo High School in Utah.

He said that they were three or four weeks into a new school year when a student came into Dr. Collett's classroom and announced he was transferring into the art class. Dr. Collett didn't question him but accepted his transfer sheet and assigned him to a seat. A few days later another student came to his art class with her transfer sheet. That was highly unusual but he said nothing until a third transferee reported to him.

He called the three newly transferred students into the hall and asked what was going on. All three were from the same mathematics class and their math teacher had told them he was arranging for their transfer into art—"where they could use their hands because he didn't believe they could use their head!"

Dr. Collett had the three transferees return to their seats, and then marched down the hall to the math room. The math teacher was writing a problem on the blackboard while explaining the process. Dr. Collett strode into the classroom, picked up the math teacher by his tie and collar with his left hand, lifting him off the floor. True! Then he said, "Your three math students are returning to your class today. You have been hired to teach them, so do it! And just remember (and he held his right hand in front of the math teacher's face) these hands don't do anything the mind doesn't tell them to do!"

Then Dr. Collett returned to the art room, sending the three students back to the math class and waited for the repercussions he fully anticipated, expecting the school office to demand an explanation for his actions. No such call came but the situation was the main topic of conversation among students and faculty for at least a week or so.

Hopefully the math teacher learned that acquiring art skills does take a mind.

As an art teacher, I can teach students to draw, paint, compose, design, use colors, appreciate art, do linear and aerial perspective accurately, letter with excellent legibility, do calligraphy, create good cartoons, etc., if the students are interested in acquiring those skills. And, I might add, it is fascinating to see how interested in art they become as they recognize how much they are learning and the many applications that knowledge has.

Years later, while I was teaching at Bountiful Senior High School, the principal wanted his daughter, Lee Ann, to enroll in one of my art classes. She reported to class the first day with a pronounced frown on her face. She did not want to take art instruction. In fact, she told me so—with tears in her eyes.

Times change.

As Lee Ann listened to instructions and watched my demonstrations, she began to enjoy art class. After high school graduation she went on to study art in a university. Today she is the long-time director of a major art school in an eastern state!

Happily, quite a number of my students made art their career, and *all* learned to see what others merely look at.

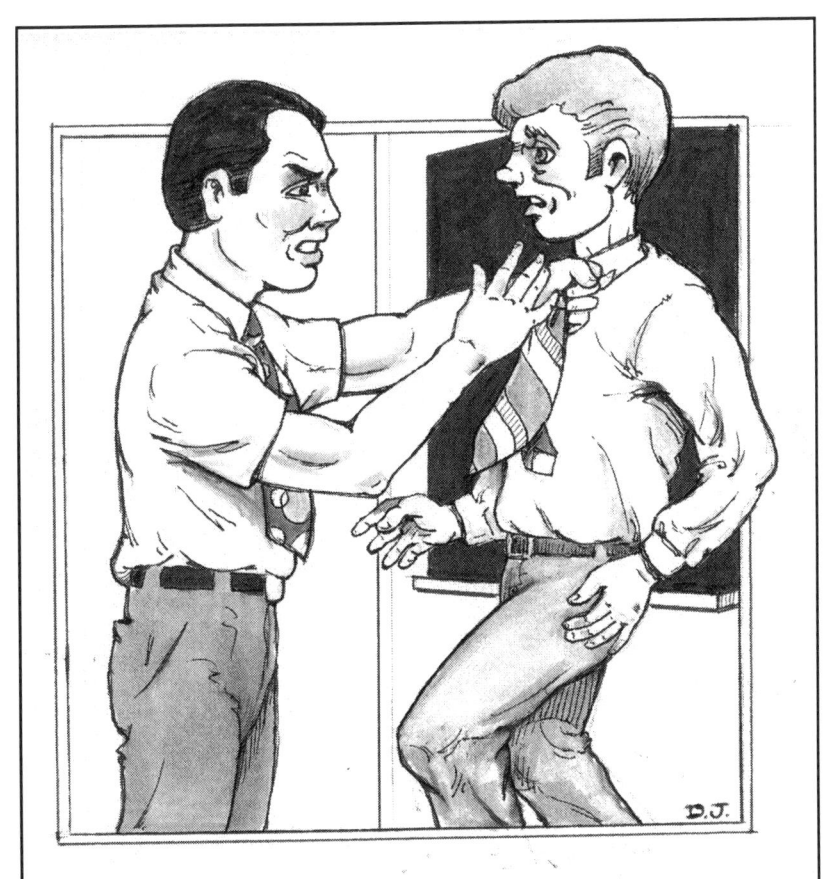

"These hands don't do anything the mind doesn't tell them to do."

The Professor's Daughter

◆

A Weber College professor had a daughter whom members of the Alpha Rho Omega Fraternity found interesting, gorgeous, intriguing, fascinating, charming, captivating, mesmerizing, and a few other adjectives that perhaps haven't been invented yet. Especially when, as a member of the college swim and diving team, she donned a fabulous swimsuit to practice in the school's pool.

Talk about a gold rush! Or Miss America! When the word spread, Alpha Rho Omega members ran from every location to serve as observers. Along with others!

When a fleeting thought crossed the cunning and creative mind of this writer, a letter was typed on fraternity letterhead stationery and mailed to the young lady in question. It read:

    Dear Miss "Smith,"

    Congratulations! You have just been selected as "The person with whom we would most enjoy being stranded on a cloud!"

    Your prize is a flight around the Great Salt Lake Valley: Ogden, Brigham City, Salt Lake City, Provo, the Great Salt Lake, Antelope Island, and the Wasatch Range.

    We suggest an early morning flight when the air is calm and the skies clear.

To schedule your *prize flight* please contact our fraternity's pilot, Don Jardine, at this number: 555-4444.

When the pretty young thing telephoned, obviously thrilled by the "award," we scheduled a Saturday morning flight. I quickly arranged for a new Cessna to be ready for us at Ogden Air Park.

The day before this eagerly-awaited event, having no car, I arranged to use my parents' automobile. And I can assure you, it hadn't been cleaned, polished and perfumed so well in its long history!

Being very careful to arrive on time (right to the second), I rang the girl's doorbell. She greeted me excitedly and actually ran to the car. She even had a camera to record this wonderful adventure.

At the airport, I checked the Cessna with great care, explaining everything as the girl anxiously awaited getting seated, strapped in (which I courteously did for her) and off the ground, into the wild blue yonder.

Fully aware that this was her first flight, I very carefully made every move (lift-off, banking, ascending etc.) as smoothly as possible.

We flew over her parents' home, where they stood, waving, on their front lawn.

We crossed over the college, circled Ogden, then headed north toward Brigham City.

Up to that point I was really patting myself on the back. This beautiful girl was having a blast, the time of her life!

Or—was she?

Why was she turning pale? With a tint of green!

I handed a "passenger flight bag" to her just in time.

My flight plan had changed very quickly! We headed back to the airport, and she seemed even more anxious to get her feet on the ground than she had been, initially, to fly!

Need I point out—that flight was my undoing. I'm sure she avoided me thenceforth and forever. My efforts to convince her there was no need for embarrassment were to no avail.

Regretfully, I had out-tricked myself.

Incidentally, I never again made such an award.

How I Met an Angel

Alpha Rho Omega, a major fraternity on Ogden's Weber College campus, invited me to become a member. I accepted, pleased because several good friends had already joined and others soon would.

One summer evening, several fraternity brothers suggested we go to Lagoon, a popular amusement park in Farmington, located between Ogden and Salt Lake City.

As we strolled down the park's midway, stopping at several of the attractions, we came upon the Merry-Go-Round. The girl in the ticket booth was just being relieved for a brief break and the reliever, a pretty redhead, attracted the attention of some Alpha Rho men. I stood to one side, listening to their banter.

One fellow asked the girl, "Is this ride dangerous?"

Without hesitation she responded, "No, we strap little boys on."

Her comment amused me—so I took my own notes when the joker learned the girl's name and address from a nearby Lagoon employee.

When I returned home from the amusement park, my mother asked where I'd been. I replied, "I went to Lagoon with some Alpha Rho brothers—and I met the girl I'm going to marry." Oh sure!

Carol Wood was a 15½-year-old high school student at that time, yet carried the responsibilities of Lagoon's assistant office manager and cashier.

I was almost 19 years old, a Marine Corps veteran and in college.

During the next four years, while waiting for Carol to "grow up," I wrote to her several times, often illustrating the envelope. We became good pen pals.

Envelope to Miss Carol Wood, 1949

I drove to Farmington to see her and met her family: delightful parents, two brothers and a sister. We dated three or four times before I let her know I had plans for our future. And I called her "Angel."

Carol's older brother had been a Marine in the Pacific during World War II, and his wife had also been in the Corps. That helped, but I believe the real clincher was her revered brother's name—he is another Don! (and author of the Foreword for this book).

Envelope to Miss Carol Wood, 1950

Years after our marriage, Carol, my Angel, sat quietly in our car one Sunday as we returned home from church. After several minutes of silence she said, "Oh Don, I'm so embarrassed." I asked why and she explained, "While you were outside of Sunday School class today, we were talking about angels, and the teacher asked if anybody had ever seen one. Before I knew it, the words came out of my mouth, 'My husband lives with one!'"

My angel and me

Very atypical for my humble wife. But she spoke the truth. Friendly, charitable, personable, lovely, intelligent—and always my Angel.

Piloting a Stinson "Flying Station Wagon"

A job clinic was held at the University of Utah for one day following graduation. There were very few contracts offered to prospective art teachers and most of those jobs were out of state.

Following interviews with five representatives of high schools, four located outside Utah, I went home discouraged. That soon changed upon receiving a telephone call advising me I was selected by the only Utah high school offering employment to teach art. Juab High School, located in Nephi, wanted me to teach art—and biology, civics and general science!

Two or three weeks before school was scheduled to begin for the fall semester, I drove to Nephi, checked out the high school, and looked for a place to live. A fellow faculty member told me his widowed mother was offering room and board for one. That was fortuitous and I was pleased when she accepted me. Her lovely brick home was only two blocks from Juab High School (grades 9-12).

One of the first people I met in Nephi was Bill Jones (not his real name), the city's postmaster. He had heard I too was an aviation enthusiast, and he owned his own airplane, a Stinson "Flying Station Wagon." Bill and I spent some time together and found we enjoyed the same things: flying, fishing, hunting, photography, and swimming.

Three weeks into the new school year, Bill came to me with a long face. As a member of a military reserve unit, he was being re-called into service and would soon leave for Korea! He was told he should plan to be overseas for a minimum of twelve months.

Bill didn't want to leave his plane in storage for that long, so he decided to sell it. He asked, "Don, would you please fly my plane to Salt Lake City on weekends until it is sold?"

"Would I? Absolutely!" Even though I had never before flown a Stinson.

Bill planned to advertise his plane in Salt Lake City and Ogden newspapers, making it available to prospective buyers for test flight. I would fly from Nephi to Salt Lake City, check the flying license and log book of each pilot wanting to fly the plane, and then if the plane wasn't sold, fly it back to Nephi.

Every Friday, immediately after teaching my final class of the day, I'd drive to the airport, remove the plane from its hangar, park my car inside, and fly to Salt Lake City. Sunday evenings I'd fly the plane back to Nephi, teach for another week, and repeat that weekend schedule.

I had been driving from Nephi to Ogden every weekend anyway, so this saved a tiresome drive and enabled me to add quite a few hours to my private pilot's log book. Those hours weren't just to and from—several of the prospective buyers preferred to have me accompany them on their trial flights rather than fly solo in an airplane they hadn't flown before. For some, that was a good idea!

My parents lived near the Ogden Air Park, where I'd learned to fly. My fiancée could often arrange to be in Ogden on weekends. It was a perfect arrangement.

Glen Collins, a fellow faculty member, had been searching for a home he could rent so his wife and two young daughters, still living in Ogden, could join him. Rental homes in Nephi were scarce, so Glen often drove to Ogden on weekends too. When he learned I was flying back and forth, he asked if he could accompany me. I agreed and he phoned his wife to suggest she stay by the phone Friday evening. He would call her from the airport so she could pick him up.

I believe the student body and faculty of Juab High School was abuzz about our first flight together. Most of them "knew" we wouldn't make it because the wind that day was near hurricane velocity. Nobody would fly in that weather!

Fall plowing of the farms had been underway for some time and the unexpectedly strong wind filled the skies with dust. In fact, visibility was extremely limited.

There was nobody at the airport that day. Glen helped me move the aircraft from its hangar following my pre-flight checks. Then he parked my car inside and closed and locked the hangar doors while I started the plane's engine.

Glen climbed aboard the plane and I directed it into the wind for take-off. But a take-off run was hardly necessary. The wind lifted the plane off the taxi-way and we were airborne!

Banking the plane soon after leaving the ground, I was able to quickly lift it above the telephone poles and wires bordering the airport, and I headed north.

Climbing very high was inadvisable. I could hardly see the ground directly below from an altitude above 400 feet! And horizontal visibility was less.

I had hundreds of hours of flight time experience, but this flight was really a major piloting test. Although I had complete confidence, I was concerned about a large hill ahead, located at the south end of Utah Lake.

Quickly figuring our speed (over the ground) and the time we'd been in the air, I climbed to a safe height to clear the hill. I kept the necessary compass heading until I was certain we had passed that obstacle. And I was right. The visibility was excellent over Utah Lake, and Provo could be seen miles ahead.

Glen was not an experienced flyer. He felt a sudden urge to empty his stomach. Opening his window, he was successful in relieving himself outside the plane—but lost his new eyeglasses! They have long resided with the fishes in the depths of Utah Lake.

Approaching Provo Airport and needing to land for fuel, I could see the windsocks and knew I'd have to put the plane down in a crosswind.

I circled the airport, and entered the traditional traffic pattern to land. The airport manager, legendary aviation expert Art Mortenson, rushed from his office to his nearby pick-up. His teenage son was close behind.

I was delighted to see Art drive his truck parallel to the runway I was about to land on, his son on the running board.

As my plane's tires touched the landing strip, Art moved his truck under the plane's wing. His son reached up, held onto the wing tip and safely counteracted the effects of the crosswind while I slowed the plane down from its 70+ mph landing speed.

The plane was quickly fueled and as I prepared to take off, we noticed an elderly couple standing near the airport office. The man had his arm around his wife's shoulders and stood with a worried look as she constantly wrung her hands and audibly whimpered.

Art explained, "See that Taylorcraft circling the airport? That is their son. He attends Utah Agricultural College in Logan and flies home every weekend. He's made six or seven landing attempts so far!"

I asked Art's son to get a large piece of cardboard—or anything else I could write on—and something with which I could write.

When those items were provided, I wrote in large letters: "USE POWER TO LAND."

Novice pilots of light aircraft are taught to decrease power as they near touchdown. In a wind, power is necessary to maintain control. This pilot didn't know that.

I took off without any problem and didn't learn the results of my four words on a poster board until I saw Art again. The young pilot made a safe landing. Using power.

Glen pointed out that it would soon be dark. Leaving Provo Airport still heading north for Salt Lake City, I climbed the plane to 1500 feet and leveled off just as the first large, wet snowflakes hit the windshield!

Passing over Point of the Mountain and Utah's State Prison, we could see the bright lights below and those of Salt Lake City ahead. I had running lights blinking on the plane, but no operative radio.

Crossing over Temple Square at the North end of the city, we could see the State Capitol Building below our right wing. Barely! Snow was clinging to the windshield as we continued our flight along the west side of the Wasatch Mountains.

Well acquainted with the area, I descended to follow lights from traffic on the highway to Ogden, our destination.

Ahead, to the Northwest, I could easily see gigantic Hill Air Force Base with its long, wide, well-lit runways. It was lit up like a small city, and was it ever inviting! However, especially with no way to communicate intention or request to land, I knew the military officials would be unhappy with any civilian pilot using their facilities without authorization. And I was not going to do so, and possibly lose my pilot's license.

Continuing past Hill Air Force Base, I banked the plane west and quickly identified Ogden Air Park just across Weber Canyon from the north end of a Hill Air Force Base major runway.

My sister Lola Patterson and her family lived in a home that was below me.

I made a low-level pass to determine conditions at Ogden Air Park. There was a 60-watt night light in the office but no other light. The airport had closed before noon that day due to heavy snowfall.

High tension lines bordered the airport on its east side, a large open field west of the runways was covered by Volkswagen-sized boulders, a large gravel pit sat at the north end and huge Weber Canyon (with river and highway) bordered the south end adjacent to Hill Air Force Base.

Any one of those things should deter a pilot from landing there after dark, with no lights, in a heavy blizzard. But I had made hundreds of landings at that airport and Glen and I could easily walk from there to my parents' home in nearby Washington Terrace.

Snow on the runway was more than a foot deep. We had just set down and were taxiing toward the office and tie-down ramps when Glen asked, "When are we going to land?" He couldn't see through the snow-covered windows.

I replied, "We *have* landed."

Then he asked, "But when are we going to be on the ground?"

"Glen," I replied, "we *are* on the ground. We've landed."

He was happier than I believed was warranted. I'd been quite busy and wasn't aware that Glen was under unbelievable stress.

We tied the Stinson down, very securely, and then hiked through the snow to my parents' home where Glen called his wife for transport to their home. She was unhappy with us—but grateful to have her husband back safe.

I slept in the next morning. My mother awakened me to take a telephone call. She said, "Don, Big Spence is on the phone."

I struggled out of bed and went to the phone.

"Jardine, did you fly a large Stinson in here last night?"

When I acknowledged that I had he let out a war whoop. He and five other pilots had been sitting around the stove in the airports' office, discussing an airplane that hadn't been there when they closed the airport the previous day. And it had been snowing, non-stop, for many hours.

Big Spence had said, "I know who flew that plane in here."

The other pilots laughed.

Big Spence said, "I'll bet each of you ten dollars I know who flew that plane here."

To me, he said, "I just made fifty bucks!"

An Unmilitary View of Saipan

From a purely objective point of view, Saipan is a beautiful island of approximately seventy-two square miles. It has a nearly perfect climate, a mountain spine lengthwise down its center, exotic palm trees, white sand beaches and an incomparably beautiful underwater world.

During my three months service as a combat swimming instructor for the Second Marine Division, I took every opportunity to dive in deep, clear water to swim among the fishes and coral. Both were fantastically colorful and the fish were of countless varieties, sizes, shapes, and markings. Many swam in schools, some of which hid between spines of coral when they were threatened. It was an underwater heaven!

Years after the war I described that heaven to my bride and wanted to share its beauties with her. I took her to Catalina Island off the coast of California. There we boarded a glass-bottom boat and went sightseeing. *Au contraire.* It was like seeing a forest—after the fire. Or you could say it was like watching television or a movie in black and white after experiencing them in radiant Technicolor. There was a huge, disappointing difference in everything compared to the tropical underwater world of the Mariana Islands.

Nightmares

◆

We had endured many air raids during the war, but the one on December 7, 1944 (third anniversary of the Pearl Harbor attack) when the Jap Zero attempted to strafe us[4], and the one where the kamikaze plane was diving directly toward me on the ship deck on Okinawa invasion day[5] were the only raids that really seemed personal.

I was covered by coral road dust from the machine gun bullets fired by the strafing Jap Zero on Saipan. The United States Air Force P-38 fighter pilot was my hero that day.

On Okinawa Invasion Day, the Jap pilot of that kamikaze plane was my hero. He suddenly opted to crash into the ship just beyond ours, sparing my life.

One of my nightmares finds me in an airplane, diving toward the earth in flames. I can always see others in the plane, sometimes Americans but usually Japanese. I saw many planes fall to earth in flames but I associate these Jap Zero fighter planes with my dreams.

In those nightmares the fear of a diving plane is severe because I believe there is nothing below, on, or above God's green earth more terrifying than a plane flying over three hundred miles an hour and firing eight machine guns, headed for you. The plane roars, the machine guns chatter, bullets

---

4 "Same Day, Same Month, Different Year" at page 177.
5 "Okinawa Invasion" at page 117.

whine, empty cartridge cases scream as they descend, and there is nothing a person can do for defense or concealment if he is in the open.

A fighter plane carries only one person, so I am unable to figure out why, in my nightmares, I see myself and others in the flaming plane.

Of course, I have nightmares about engagements with the enemy, including some of the engagements described in this book. Especially when the Jap soldier I had shot later faced his captors, requested death, and bowed.[6] But there are more. Many more.

When I married, my frequent nightmares still caused me to scream and thrash around before I finally awakened. My bride told me so! Those episodes frightened her and caused me to be apprehensive about sleep.

Fortunately, she was very understanding...and the nightmares, over time, became less frequent. But, after sixty-eight years, they recur several times each month.

If I could put them into factually descriptive words, you wouldn't believe them. It is horrific baggage to live with.

---

6   "In the Sugar Cane—the Most Dramatic Scene of my Life" at page 151 above.

Shots Fired

♦

On duty as Farmington, Utah's City Marshal, I was talking with the cashier at the entrance to Lagoon Amusement Park's automobile parking lot.

It was a hot summer day, the kind people seemed to prefer for a visit to Lagoon and its world-class outdoor swimming pool. Cars were streaming in.

During a lull in the traffic, a large sedan barreled down Lagoon Lane at a recklessly high speed. I wrote its license plate number down before it screeched to a stop at the cashier's booth.

The driver, a teenager, called out, "Do we have to pay to get into this place?"

When the cashier said yes, the youngster swore and floored the gas pedal, spinning the car around, and sped toward Farmington.

Though I was in uniform, the driver had ignored me. I did, however, soon become the center of attention.

A family was approaching Lagoon's entrance as the large sedan, with four boisterous young men inside, careened toward them.

There was a resounding crash as the two vehicles collided, head on.

Knowing the young driver's frame of mind, I ran to his car, aimed the muzzle of my .38 caliber police revolver between his eyes, and said, "Back up slowly and park this car. You are under arrest."

He put the sedan in reverse, backed up, then put it in forward gear and attempted to run me over!

Hurling myself away and avoiding the car, I then jumped up from my prone position on the gravel and fired three shots at the rapidly fleeing vehicle's left rear tire.

I missed.

As Lagoon employees and bystanders rushed to help three small children and their parents from the family's badly damaged car, I ran to Lagoon's nearby office and telephoned the Highway Patrol.

I informed them of the situation and gave them the offender's license plate number and automobile description. I was told that that car had been reported stolen, and that there was an all-points bulletin out for the arrest of its occupants.

They were wanted for several violations in addition to automobile theft.

I added reckless driving, leaving the scene of an accident, flight to avoid prosecution, disobeying a police officer, and *attempted murder!*

Nearly an hour passed before a State Highway Patrol officer, a friend of mine, came to Lagoon to let me know that the offending driver and his three teenage companions were in jail. He had located them and their stalled, stolen vehicle high up on a nearby mountain road. He added, "And there were three bullet holes, very close together, just above the left rear tire."

The rest of the story makes me wonder about justice. Yes, the car was stolen. However, the report came from the driver's father—who happened to be a very wealthy and influential resident of a nearby city. He dropped the stolen car charge.

A judge heard the case, agreed to drop the stolen car charge and, at the request of an attorney, decided to drop all charges upon receiving proof that the four boys, each one seventeen years old, had enlisted in the U.S. Military!

All four joined the Navy.

The driver's father agreed to pay all expenses incurred by the victim family.

This incident was widely promulgated for a week or so, then it seemed forgotten.

I, for one, will never forget it. I still remember the sneering, haughty, contemptuous looks I received from four young men who had gotten their adult lives off to a very bad start.

Trophy Buck

◆

In Washington, D.C., cherry blossom time is a big event. In New Orleans, Mardi Gras is a big event. In Pasadena, California, it's the Rose Parade. In Utah, it's *deer hunting season.*

Jerry Thompson, a dear friend, was employed and unable to hunt except on weekends. My situation was the same, so we hunted deer every Saturday. Unsuccessfully.

However, Utah had a brief post-season hunt that year. Great!

Jerry and I planned a hunt in the high Uinta Mountains for the first Saturday. I agreed to drive.

Friday evening I made every necessary preparation to go into a remote area above Kamas. Very early Saturday morning, I put on my long-johns, two pairs of pants, a heavy flannel shirt, a sweat shirt, warm padded jacket, good gloves, heavy socks, waterproof boots, and a fur-lined cap with earmuffs. (I hate the cold.)

I waddled out to my previously packed Ford, drove to Jerry's house, and waited for him to join me in my slowly warming car. It was 4:00 a.m.

And I waited.

There wasn't a light on in Jerry's house. Where was he?

Concerned about awakening his wife so very early on an extremely cold winter morning, I plowed through the snow to Jerry's bedroom window and tapped on the frosted glass. No response.

I tapped again. No result.

I tapped louder. Finally, Jerry came to the window and indicated I should meet him at the front door.

I did.

Jerry was still in his pajamas! He said, "I'm not feeling very well this morning, Don. You go on without me." Then he added, "Good luck."

Well, I was ready to hunt, so I did.

My destination, east of Salt Lake City, was quite a distance from our homes in Bountiful. Over icy roads, I persevered. Well above the small town of Kamas, I pulled off the highway onto a small, unplowed and untraveled rural road. Soon I arrived at a half-moon drive where I could park my car without interfering with the passage of any driver attempting to go farther into that heavily snowpacked high Uinta wilderness.

With the stubborn determination characteristic of the Jardine family, I pulled myself through deep snow by grasping the tops of abundant sagebrush.

After struggling upward for an hour or so, I stopped to rest. Suddenly, bursting downhill from a stand of pine trees located above me, a huge mule deer buck ran through the snow toward a ridge about two hundred yards away. Snow flew in every direction around him as he ran as fast as possible.

I quickly raised my rifle, knowing I had time for only one shot before that very large deer crossed over the ridge, into the deep ravine beyond. With a cold-numbed trigger finger, I squeezed off that shot as the buck disappeared over the ridge.

Forcing my way through the snow, I reached the place where I had last seen the buck, hoping to find some evidence that my bullet had found its mark.

Looking down into the ravine, among the tops of sagebrush peeking above the deep snow, I saw a twig. A branch. No, it was an antler! Yippee!

Hurrying down the steep incline, I located my buck.

Field dressing the deer (which is best for tasty venison—and sheds many pounds to ease transport of the deer) I tied a rope around the base of its large antlers and began my arduous trek back to the car.

It took a long time to drag that heavy buck through the snow, and through sagebrush which seemed to grasp the antlers—the antlers I was determined to protect and to keep intact.

Upon finally reaching my car, I opened the trunk and attempted to lift the deer inside. Sure!

Hearing a car approaching, I left the half-moon drive and stood in the road, flagging down a pickup truck driven by a deer hunter with his wife beside him.

The driver pulled to a stop, opened his door and shouted, "Where is it?"

He assumed my car had slid off the ice- and snow-covered road, and that I needed help getting it back on.

"My car is in this half-moon drive and I'd appreciate your help getting a deer into the trunk," I replied.

"Hell yes! I'd like to see the deer one man can't lift into a car!"

When my new friend saw the trophy deer, he exclaimed, "My ___! Where did you get that, and how did you get it to your car?"

He took one end of the deer while I held the other. We tried, with difficulty, to get the deer into the trunk.

The man's wife, a hefty lady, leaned against the car, laughing at us. Her husband didn't appreciate it. He said, "Alice, get your fat butt over here and give us a hand."

She did.

With her help we hoisted my trophy deer into the trunk—with ease!

In Salt Lake City, Zinik's Sporting Goods Store sponsored an annual Trophy Deer Contest. I entered my buck in that competition and won fishing gear prizes for having the fourth-largest deer killed in Utah that year.

Jerry was chagrined.

I was happy!

A Job Recommendation that Changed Everything

♦

This book would not be complete without mention of some very special friends. I met them all because of Arnold Friberg.

Arnold Friberg was one of my art professors at the University of Utah. After I was awarded a University of Utah gold key for illustrating the school's *Pen Magazine* and its yearbook *The Utonian,* Arnold asked me to work with him as a studio assistant.

I had to decline Arnold's offer, because I had already signed a one-year contract to teach art for Juab High School in Nephi, Utah. That was only a few weeks before Cecil B. DeMille, the famous Hollywood movie producer, signed Arnold to be the art director, designer and illustrator for the epic movie *The Ten Commandments.* Although I may have missed an opportunity there, eleven years later Arnold made another recommendation that changed my life.

At the end of my one year at Juab High School, a large new senior high school was nearing completion in Bountiful, Utah. I was asked to fill the position of art instructor. I made the wise decision to accept and was even asked to select the school's colors, to make recommendations for interior decor, and to design the art department.

Near the end of my tenth year on the Bountiful Senior High School's faculty, I began receiving long-distance telephone calls from an art school in Minneapolis, Minnesota. Actually, they were quite vexing because my classroom was on the third floor. When the loudspeaker blared, "Mr. Jardine, you have a long-distance call," I had to go to the school's office on the main floor to answer the call. I had no idea why that art school was calling me.

The caller told me that Arnold Friberg—movie art director, illustrator for a printing of the Book of Mormon, and renowned creator of many paintings of the Royal Canadian Mounted Police for the Northwest Paper Company calendars—had strongly advised that retiring director of Education Walter J. Wilwerding be replaced by Don Jardine! I was amazed.

I telephoned Arnold for an explanation. He said, "Don, it is a wonderful opportunity. Accept the job and you'll head up a department of about thirty degreed art instructors, highly professional artists, some with blue-ribbon backgrounds. You'll author art publications, meet and associate with world-famous artists, and have several travel experiences every year. I suggest you accept their offer."

Frankly, their offer was a financial disappointment, considering the increased cost of living in Minneapolis.

I asked Arnold about Minneapolis. He replied with a brief description that was remarkably accurate. He said it's the largest small town in America.

After several phone calls, each of which required chasing down to the high school's office, I finally said, "I've never been in Minneapolis and have no interest in moving from Bountiful."

The school sent a round-trip airline ticket to me.

As the school year ended and my summer job hadn't yet begun, I flew to Minneapolis. It was a pleasant experience, but I couldn't decide on my own. My wife, Carol, and I were a team.

She had to help with such an important, life-changing decision. I told the school this, and they sent two round-trip tickets. Carol accompanied me on my second trip to Minneapolis. We were chauffeured, dined, entertained, and coaxed.

After promising to make a decision within two weeks, Carol and I returned to Utah. We sought counsel from family members, our bishop, close friends, and through prayer. Finally, Carol and I decided we'd go to Minneapolis for a year or two, and then we would return to Utah.

That was the end of June, 1962. Minneapolis would be our home for the next forty-five years!

Walter J. Wilwerding was the person I replaced at Art Instruction Schools. He had been director for 30 years. As it turned out, my tenure in that position exceeded Walters!

I was well acquainted with the works of Walter J. Wilwerding, especially those featured in *National Geographic Magazine* that had been researched on African safaris. It did surprise me to learn that he also had designed the greyhound for the Greyhound Bus Company.

Meeting the staff of Art Instruction Schools was impressive, and I was amazed at how large the school was. The Bureau of Engraving is the mother company for the art school, which has an unparalleled history for their more than one-hundred-year-old "Draw Me" advertising campaign. I was destined to create twenty-eight cartoon characters for that advertising. Some became famous, not only in the United States but in several foreign countries.

After the school appointed me editor of its magazine, *The Illustrator*, I reviewed new art books for each issue, enabling me to add to my fast-growing list of friends, as Arnold Friberg had predicted. The artists I met through the years include: Les

Kouba; John Clymer; Charles Schulz; Donald Teague; Ken Carlson; Bob Kuhn; Jim Smith; Charles Gravem; Walter Wilwerding; Ward Kimball; Mort Walker; Farrell R. Collett; Floyd Gottfredson; Melvin C. Warren; Roy Kerswill; Wayne Meineke; George Pollard; Jim Killen; George Schelling; Joseph S. Venus; Frederic Taubes; Barbara Schwinn; Charles Murphy; Richard Lack; Don Koestner; Lu Fuller; Howard Sanden; Clair Fry; Tore Asplund; Claude Croney; Clark Bronson; Charles Hawes; D. Omer Seamon; Frieda Rich; Gustav Rehberger; Paul VanDemark; and many others.

When Walter Foster Publishing Co. asked me to author and illustrate a book on cartooning, *Creating Cartoon Characters* resulted. I asked Charles Schulz, creator of "Peanuts" comic strip, to write the introduction, and he graciously complied.

A second cartoon book was requested, so I authored and illustrated *Creating Cartoon Animals*. Mort Walker, creator of "Beetle Bailey" and "Hi and Lois," agreed to supply the introduction. This book was later translated into Russian and published in Russia. (The Russians never kept their agreements. My U.S. publisher and I never received copies nor royalties. However, Matt Rowley, now my granddaughter's husband, served a church mission there and purchased Russian versions of my book for me.)

Charles "Sparky" Schulz, creator of "Peanuts"

♦

While I was editor of *The Illustrator*, the international art magazine published by Art Instruction Schools, I wrote an article about my friend Charles M. Schulz, the creator of "Peanuts" comic strip. The following is an excerpt:

"When I joined Art Instruction Schools in 1962, I was very naïve and presumptuous. I actually wrote to Charles Schulz asking him to autograph and personalize six 'Peanuts' books I sent to him. Typically, Sparky wrote in each book exactly as requested and returned them to me! We've been good friends ever since.

"In 1968, Sparky learned my wife Carol and I were scheduled to attend the National Art Education Association's annual conference in New York City. He telephoned and asked if we'd like to attend his opening stage play 'You're a Good Man, Charlie Brown.' Would we! Of course! We were overwhelmed by the invitation.

"When we arrived at the theater's box office and gave our names, we were presented with two complimentary tickets set aside for us at Sparky's request. And it was a great show!

"We were absolutely charmed by a delightfully funny, warm, simple, and highly entertaining cast of two young ladies and four young men, plus one musician. (Gary Burghoff, known by everyone for his role as 'Radar' in the popular M.A.S.H. Television series, played Charlie Brown.)

"It was an unforgettable evening. One difficult to describe because it was so unlike the shows one usually sees in New York. No special stage sets or costuming. Few props. No orchestra. Simple...but captivating.

"The cast was given a standing ovation at the end of their evening performance and nobody out-clapped Carol or me.

"In 1969, *A Boy Named Charlie Brown* opened at Radio City Music Hall in New York City. It was the first animated movie shown there in over 20 years, and it broke every major record of the Music Hall's 37-year history, including the greatest advance sales, the greatest single day, and the greatest single week. Its success was based in part, no doubt, on Charles Schulz's well-earned reputation for providing wholesome family entertainment.

"Schulz's TV specials such as *You're in Love, Charlie Brown; A Charlie Brown Thanksgiving*, and *A Charlie Brown Christmas* have been seen by millions. The latter earned an Emmy Award and a Peabody Award while the preceding received another Emmy.

"Charlie Brown (the real person that inspired Schulz to develop the famous character) was a close friend to all of us here at the school and often dropped in for a chat. He helped judge several Annual Art Competitions and other student art contests. In addition, he had a deep interest in every improvement the school made in teaching young people to draw, paint and cartoon. But the most memorable events I associate with 'Good Ol' Charlie Brown' were during our Christmas parties when Charlie played the piano for Frieda Rich (the inspiration for

Schulz's Frieda character) as she mimicked and danced to the record 'All I Want for Christmas Is My Two Front Teeth.'

"Had Sparky been present for those performances they would quite probably have inspired ideas for his comic strip, because you've never seen anything as funny as Frieda with two front teeth blacked out, wearing a long flannel nightgown and acting with the precision of a seasoned comedienne! It was truly side-splitting fun.

"Sparky says finding an idea is the most important part of developing a comic strip so that task comes first. He often sits at his desk gazing out a window as if day-dreaming but, in reality, he is searching his mind, his thoughts and memories for ideas. Often he doodles on a small pad hoping one of his Snoopy, Lucy or Charlie Brown drawings will spark a humorous idea. Once he has a gag in mind, he can finish the drawing and inking of a daily strip in an hour. Sparky produces six daily strips each week and devotes a full day to drawing a Sunday strip. His tools and materials are few and simple: a soft pencil, four or five pens, a small brush and black ink. Lettering is always rendered first, then the characters are drawn, and finally the balloons enclosing the lettering are added.

"Schulz keeps his preliminary pencil work surprisingly simple, preferring instead to work directly with pen and ink. Unlike some cartoonists he never varies the size of the panels that make up a daily strip. Each original panel measures 5" wide by 5" deep.

"Ideas, sketches, lettering and inking...and another *Peanuts* strip is ready.

"We're proud of Charles 'Sparky' Schulz and happy to be his friends."

Judging of Art

Over the many years of my career as an artist, I have judged literally dozens of art shows and competitions: local, county, state, regional, national, and international.

As a rule, to preclude tie votes, I joined two other judges. We made our own evaluations, then sat together and compared our choices.

Submissions to these events were usually based upon special parameters such as age limits, subject matter, mediums used, and so on.

Professor Farrell R. Collett, a master art instructor, set the pattern for my selections. He taught his art students at Weber College in Ogden, Utah, to consider sizes, shapes, textures, colors, balance, repetition, continuity, novelty, contrast, simplicity, accuracy, perspective (linear and aerial), unity, the five values of light (highlight, halftone, reflected light, shadow edge, and cast shadow), proportions, creativity, emphasis and subordination, leading lines, etc.

Art is complex.

A majority of "artists" (and even art judges) are unaware of these considerations.

When someone says, "I'm a self-taught artist," I usually think, "That goes without mentioning. Self-taught? Yes. Artist? No!"

A number of my fellow art judges have said, "I selected this painting because it spoke to me."

In sixty-five years of judging art, I have never had a painting *speak to me.*

Personal preference dictates the winners of most art competitions. It is regrettable that many superior paintings, etchings, bronzes, etc. are overlooked due to the limited training (education) of a judge or judges.

We've all heard, "I don't know much about art, but I know what I like." That is *good.* Paintings created by well-trained artists who incorporate good art principles are of lesser value to any collector if they don't depict in a way that stimulates pleasure.

However, in my opinion, it is the duty of a real judge of art to make winning selections based upon the *merits* of entries rather than by being spoken to!

Determination! Art Competition for the Handicapped

◆

For fifteen consecutive years, I was one of three judges who selected winners in Sister Kenny Institute's Annual Art Competition for the Handicapped. When an important business trip to New York City seemed to conflict with one competition, I telephoned Margaret Anderson, chairwoman of Kenny Institute's Auxiliary, to explain the situation.

My return to Minneapolis was scheduled for art judging day, but the time was still undetermined.

Margaret expressed disappointment, stating that the other two judges had been selected, but she would ask a Kenny staff member to take my place if it became necessary (to preclude possible tie selections).

Landing at Twin Cities International Airport from New York, I telephoned Margaret. She said the judging was about to begin and asked me to come directly from the airport and serve as the third judge. She also said, "We have added something new to this year's competition. A talented young handicapped artist has donated a small oil painting which will be raffled off to begin building an art scholarship fund. Would you like to purchase a one-dollar ticket?"

I replied, "I'll take fifty tickets."

After the judging, the winning raffle ticket was selected from a barrel containing thousands of tickets. It was one of mine!

The 9-by-12-inch oil painting I won is entitled, "Winter on the Farm." It is a gem and no winner could have been more delighted, more appreciative, nor more able to use it so effectively as an incentive for hundreds of university art students.

Twenty-four-year-old Glen A. Fowler had been a previous winner in Kenny Institute's art competitions, in the category of drawing and painting with mouth! (Other categories included drawing and painting with feet, with attachments to wrists, to elbow, and to shoulder). Glen is a paraplegic.

As I shared the painting with students of every subsequent art class I taught for the University of Minnesota, they probably examined it with a question—why? It is a nicely executed, beautiful little oil painting—so?

After every student had looked at the painting, I had them pass it around again, to look at the back. None of them had thought to turn it over. If they had, they would have seen the winning raffle ticket attached, and the information "Painted by Glen A. Fowler with a brush held between his teeth!"

If Glen was able to develop such art skills, what should be possible for every art student, using their good right or left hand?

P.S. Margaret Anderson, a polio victim, spent many years in an iron lung, then with a respirator. Even so, creating art by holding pencils, pens and brushes between her teeth, she graduated from Art Instruction Schools' home study course. I was present when she was awarded her graduation certificate.

Determination!

Who's Flying a Jet T-33? Me!

♦

I have occasionally read articles about public elementary and middle school teachers experiencing flight in U.S. Air Force jets. Ostensibly, those experiences were to assist educators as they encouraged students to set good study goals.

Reasoning that I was an educator, that I had founded and instructed a senior high school aviation club with a new Cessna 180 aircraft, and was a taxpayer in good standing with the I.R.S., I decided to contact a few influential friends in Washington, D.C. I requested their help arranging for me to take a ride in a jet.

With good results.

It was a pleasant surprise to receive a letter from the commanding officer of an Air National Guard unit stationed at Hill Air Force Base in Ogden, Utah. Upon request from Air Force headquarters in the nation's capitol, he set a date and time for my "orientation flight" in a T-33 jet (a two-place trainer with dual controls). Great!

On the appointed day, I was on time for the treasured flight.

However, the procedure was a bit more complicated than I had anticipated. I filled out required official forms which relieved the Air Force of any and all responsibility. I supplied answers and information for many questions. Upon completing those forms, I was interviewed by a flight officer interested in my flying background, my health, flying club purposes, etc.

Completing an hour or so of the above, I was then given a lengthy lecture on what to do if there was an emergency, including a flame-out, use of a parachute, ejection procedures, and how to use the controls should the pilot experience a sudden health problem precluding his ability to land the aircraft.

Finally, I was fitted with a flight suit and helmet, accompanied to the plane, given "hands-on" instructions and a parachute.

I was introduced to my pilot, helped into the rear seat, strapped firmly in place, and was given a "thumbs up" as he started the powerful engine.

After a brief warm up, we began to roll toward the taxi strip that led to the assigned runway for takeoff.

Every procedure, from starting the engine, checking instruments, the warm up, and taxiing was coordinated with the control tower by radio.

Ready to board the Air Force T-33 trainer jet for a flight over the Great Salt Lake Desert

Standing on the brakes, my pilot pushed the throttle forward, read his instruments, then, with a "go" from the tower, he released the brakes and we began the takeoff run.

Personnel and buildings alongside the runway seemed to move by faster and faster as we accelerated. Then we lifted into the air and the ride became wonderfully smooth, more so than the light aircraft I was accustomed to piloting.

Flying just above the end of the runway, the plane's flight path very suddenly and unexpectedly changed from horizontal to vertical! A light plane (Piper Cub, Taylorcraft, Mooney, Ercoupe, Cessna, Stinson, Aeronca, etc.) would have quickly stalled with that action. But the jet just accelerated! I felt its great power throughout my body as I followed the pilot's movements on my set of controls.

Upon leaving Hill Air Force Base, we headed west, over the Great Salt Lake, at an altitude above 10,000 feet. The pilot then asked if I would like to take the controls and fly the jet.

Would I? Wow!

I asked the pilot about restrictions. "What can I do?"

He replied, "Anything. You're the pilot."

Well, I had always wanted to *dive* an airplane. Only shallow dives were possible in the "puddle jumpers" I was accustomed to flying. So I nosed the jet earthward, planning to go straight down for several thousand feet, then pull out of the vertical dive, relieved of the usual fear of losing the wings.

My pilot grabbed his controls and put us back into horizontal flight.

"Sorry," he said. "That was my fault. I should have let you know that pushing this plane rapidly into a dive deflects air from the air intake and often causes a flame-out. If you want to dive the plane it's OK, but push it slowly into the dive."

I did.

Surprisingly, the rest of the one-hour flight was completed with me at the controls with only one exception: The pilot asked, "Would you like to experience a 'gray-out'? Regulations won't permit me to let you 'black out,' but I can pull enough G's (force against gravity) for you to 'gray out.'" (In a gray out, one does not lose consciousness, but loses brain function to the extent he cannot properly read instruments or control the airplane.)

I agreed. The nose of the jet was pushed toward the ground below from an altitude of 20,000 feet.

As instructed, I read the whirling altimeter to my pilot over the radio as we descended like a rocket.

As we pulled out of the vertical dive, exerting several G's, I was still reading the altimeter accurately.

The pilot said, "Hell, Jardine, you can take as much as I can. I'm afraid you won't experience a 'gray-out' today."

The rest of that initial jet flight was uneventful. However, it wasn't my only T-33 ride. I later had two more, both from Hill Air Force Base.

My second jet flight required three hours preparation, most of which was repetitive of flight number one, due to new, stricter regulations.

The third flight, due to additional regulations, required almost four hours of review—instruction and preparation. However it was a fantastic flight. A real ball.

After I related my attempted "gray-out" experience to my new pilot, he suggested another try.

With him at the controls, we quickly reached 20,000 feet. Asking if I was ready, he pushed the jet's nose earthward and we had a very fast ride down nearly to the surface of Great Salt

Lake. In fact, we were near Promontory Point, famous as the location where two trains met, many years ago, completing the first rail span across the nation. And as we pulled out of that dive, the pilot had to lift the plane up to cross over the railroad tracks. We were low! But I didn't "gray-out."

I had my 35 mm twin lens reflex camera with me and, when I wasn't flying the jet, I took many photos. Then the pilot had a good idea. He used the jet's radio to ask, "Are there any birds approaching Utah?"

An immediate reply stated, "A flight of three F-101's are nearing Hill Air Force Base from Nellis A.F.B. Base in Nevada. We're at 16,000 feet on a N.N.E. Heading."

We were S.S.W. of Hill Air Force Base, in their flight path.

My pilot said, "I have a civilian pilot aboard my T-33 and he would appreciate a fly-by so he can take your picture."

The F-101 pilot said they would watch for us and suggested we climb to 18,000 feet. Their fighters were camouflaged and an interesting photo would be possible with the Utah desert for a background.

My pilot said, "Keep your eyes open for the three fighters, Jardine. Let's see which one of us can spot them first."

I'm not sure he didn't "let me win," but I reported the three F-101's first.

In formation, the three fighters passed below us. Our T-33 was in a dive, pushing 400 m.p.h., when I photographed them flying at more than 300 m.p.h. I clicked the camera's shutter. I didn't have time for a second exposure. Fortunately, all three F-101's were captured in a corner of that negative, which was easily enlarged. It proved to be a most unusual photograph, and proves the efficacy of properly applied camouflage.

Photo I took from T-33 trainer jet of three F-101 Air Force Jets over the Great Salt Lake Desert

    My three jet flights amazed me with the lack of speed awareness. Except when near a cloud, the ground, or another aircraft, there was no sensation of speed, no more so than in smaller, slower planes I had piloted. But the controls were easier to handle and it took far less time to go from point A to point B.

    The jet pilots with whom I flew were generous in allowing me to fly each of those three T-33's, over 40 minutes each time. They and the ground personnel were very pleasant, considerate, and able people.

    I loved every minute!

The King's Opening Night

When Fred and Kathy, good friends of Carol and me, suggested the four of us drive to Las Vegas for a fun weekend, we agreed immediately. We'd made that trip with them several times each year and always enjoyed it. And why not? In those days you could see top entertainers by purchasing a sandwich and a fruit punch for $1.00 each. Two dollars was the minimum cover charge per guest. A very fair price!

We had seen Abbott & Costello, Danny Kaye, Glenn Miller and his orchestra, Johnny Ray, The Beach Boys, The Mills Brothers, The Lettermen, Lionel Hampton, Pat Boone, Johnny Mathis, Sarah Vaughn, Woody Herman, The Ink Spots, Frankie Laine, Count Basie, Nat "King" Cole and several other great entertainers in the showrooms of famous Las Vegas hotels such as The Sands, Tropicana, Desert Inn, The Frontier, Golden Nugget, The Four Queens, Stardust, and others.

Upon arrival at our favorite Las Vegas motel, the manager greeted us and asked if we would like her to make show reservations for us. We admitted we hadn't yet checked to determine what shows were playing, so she gave us a booklet listing the shows playing in Las Vegas hotels that week.

"Nat 'King' Cole?!! Wow. We're in luck! That's our first choice."

She laughed and said, "You and a thousand other people. That show has been sold out for three months. It's his opening night."

I thanked her and motioned for Carol and our friends to follow me. I drove them to The Sands. We entered and went directly to the showroom. The hotel guard posted there looked us over as he slumped on his stool in the entrance way.

"You people need some help?"

I replied, "Yes, I'd like to see Nat Cole's manager," and I called him by name.

The guard stood and took an entirely different attitude.

"Do you know him?"

"I'm a friend of his and Mr. Cole."

Fred and Kathy stared in fearful awe, looking as though I was committing a major crime.

"I'll see what I can do," the guard replied, "Wait here."

When he returned, Nat "King" Cole's manager was with him.

"Hi Don! Hi Carol! You want to see the show?"

Fred and Kathy would have dropped their dentures, if they'd had any.

"Yes, but we've been told it's sold out."

"That's true, but you come back just before 8:00 and we'll take care of you."

What a night!

We returned before the show and were escorted to our table. There wasn't room for it on the showroom floor, so our friend had one placed *on stage* (in the wings)!

Not only did we see Nat "King" Cole's show, up *close*, but he came to our table after the show and we introduced him to Fred and Kathy.

A record was cut that night. It was entitled "Nat 'King' Cole: Opening Night at the Sands." It was fabulous.

And I might add, the prime rib we were served was out of this world. One of the best meals we'd ever had, and front seats to enjoy songs by our number one favorite singer. It was truly a great evening.

The motel manager asked us the following day, "What show did you folks see last night?" When I told her, she burst into laughter. "No way," she said. She did not believe us!

Perhaps she may have been convinced had she known we were friends of Nat Cole and his manager. Carol was office manager and central cashier for Lagoon Amusement Park in Farmington, Utah, her home town. She was the one entertainers saw for their pay. And I was the "bouncer" in Lagoon's ballroom, responsible for arranging breaks for the featured entertainers. Through these jobs we both became acquainted with many of America's favorite, top entertainers. They included: Nat "King" Cole; Stan Kenton; Johnny Cash; Louis "Satchmo" Armstrong; Les Brown; Billy Eckstein; Fats Domino; Tommy & Jimmy Dorsey; Duke Ellington; Count Basie; Johnny Mathis; Mel Torme; Pat Boone; Sarah Vaughn, and many others.

Grandpa!

♦

I was delightedly amazed soon after moving into my new home in Ephraim, Utah. The doorbell rang and when I opened the door, an attractive and personable young girl introduced herself. She is the daughter of neighbors and appeared a bit anxious, but determined, when she asked, "Mr. Jardine, may I call you Grandpa?"

Lindsey Bradley explained that she has grandparents on her father's and mother's side, but they live some distance away and she seldom has an opportunity to visit with them.

"And most of my friends have a grandparent they can visit. I'd like one too."

It was a big, pleasant surprise.

I replied, "Lindsey, it is certainly alright with me—*if* your parents approve."

A few days later, Lindsey returned and greeted me, "Hello Grandpa!"

Most of my grandchildren live in distant states, so it always pleases me when Lindsey visits. And that has been quite frequently because her home is only one block from mine, and her parents are now my good friends.

I have been somewhat of a Pied Piper for many children, primarily because they enjoy the drawings and cartoons I do for them. They also seem to feel close to a widower older than their own grandparents.

Girl's Second-Choice Date

◆

On an evening just prior to Halloween, my doorbell rang. I hoisted my 85-year-old body out of a comfortable recliner and made my way to the front door. There, to my surprise, was a nine-year-old neighbor girl with tears in her eyes.

I had seen this little girl several times in church and had spoken to her occasionally, but she was essentially a stranger.

After I greeted her, she said, "Mr. Jardine, tomorrow night is a Daddy Daughter Date Night. There's going to be a Halloween party. All my friends will be there...but my Daddy is out of town on a business trip." Then she began sobbing. Between spasms of heartfelt grief, she asked, "Will you take me?"

What would you have done?

I surprised myself by saying, "Sure, I'll take you." I just couldn't refuse.

The party was being held in the recreation room of a neighboring home, so transportation wouldn't be a problem. However, everyone was expected to attend in a Halloween costume.

The next day I went to Walmart and purchased the items necessary to transform myself from the neighborhood's ugly, old, fat, bald man into a Caribbean pirate: mask, hat, vest, sash, toupee, false mustache, and plastic sword! I even purchased a black, tar-like substance to visually eliminate a couple of front teeth, which, I might add, was nearly impossible to remove after my "date."

Pirate and Princess

    I escorted nine-year-old Courtney Lee, dressed as the princess she is, to the party, which was attended entirely by eight-, nine-, and ten-year-old girls with their dads. All were in costume and a great time was had by all.

Well, almost all.

Every daddy there was young enough to be my grandson. I certainly felt out of place with dads one-third my age.

However, I still own the memory of Courtney Lee, a nine-year-old girl who had changed from a tearful child into one of the happiest, most cheerful princesses at the Daddy Daughter Halloween party, accompanied by the 85-year-old Pirate.

Conclusion

In the Author's Introduction to this book, I said, "If you enjoy true adventure short stories, I promise you will love this book." I hope I fulfilled that promise.

Writing it wasn't easy, especially for a laggard who had to make copious notes whenever his aging memory brought back experiences that had been wilfully hidden for many years.

I express my sincere love, appreciation, and gratitude to all my brothers-in-arms. Every one is a hero. They loved our country and demonstrated that love by putting their life on the line—repeatedly. I owe my life to several of them. We were like brothers.

Once a Marine, always a Marine.

I would love to hear your comments.
> Don L. Jardine, Ph.D.
> 935 S 950 E
> Ephraim, Utah 84627
> DonJardine@CombatMarineAt17.com

More information at:

http://CombatMarineAt17.com

Made in the USA
Lexington, KY
10 April 2014